HAUNTED SCRANTON

AFTER DARK IN THE ELECTRIC CITY

A.C. BERNARDI

Haunted
America

Published by Haunted America
A Division of The History Press
Charleston, SC 29403
www.historypress.net

Front cover: The Lackawanna County Courthouse Building. *Photo by Olivia Bernardi.*

Back cover, top: Snyder Hall with light rays in the Scranton Cultural Center. *Courtesy of the Scranton Cultural Center at the Masonic Temple.* Bottom: George and Helen Catlin relaxing by the water. *Courtesy of the Lackawanna Historical Society.*

First published 2012

Manufactured in the United States

ISBN 978.1.60949.585.5

Library of Congress Cataloging-in-Publication Data

Bernardi, Anthony C.
Haunted Scranton : after dark in the electric city / Anthony C. Bernardi.
p. cm.
Includes bibliographical references.
ISBN 978-1-60949-585-5
1. Haunted places--Pennsylvania--Scranton. I. Title.
BF1472.U6B468 2012
133.109748'37--dc23
2012034062

Notice: The information in this book is true and complete to the best of our knowledge. It is offered without guarantee on the part of the author or The History Press. The author and The History Press disclaim all liability in connection with the use of this book.

CONTENTS

ACKNOWLEDGEMENTS

First, I would like to take a moment to thank everyone who helped me make this book (my first published work) a reality. Since I can remember, I've enjoyed countless hours reading books regarding this subject matter, but I never thought I would have the esteemed honor of authoring one myself. It is truly a dream come true.

My mother, Sarah Bernardi, showed me how wonderful life can be.

My father, Anthony Bernardi Sr., taught me the importance of working hard.

My patient and talented wife, Olivia Bernardi, is the best person I could ever dream of knowing and a great photographer, too.

The love of my three beautiful children, Evan, Owen and Gwen, helps to keep my spirit young and my imagination active.

Mary Ann Moran-Savakinus, director of the Lackawanna Historical Society and friend, thank you for your recommendation and for opening your mind to the paranormal.

All of my remaining family members and friends (you know who you are), without your love, support and encouragement, I would not be the person I am today. Thank you and God bless.

My pets, Sugar and Avon, keep me in touch with nature and remind me to enjoy the simple pleasures life has to offer.

Lastly, I would like to thank all of the departed, lost and restless souls out there still clinging to this world. For without you, a book such as this could not be written. I have felt your cold touch and have heard your distant voices. Your tragic and haunting tales teach us to enjoy and appreciate life while we still have it and help us to imagine that there can be existence beyond death. May you someday find the strength of will and ability to pass on to a better state of being.

INTRODUCTION

HOW I GOT STARTED

I never truly believed that ghosts *really do* exist until I was twenty-five years old. Up until that point, I was just an optimistic skeptic who loved the darker side of history. From the time I was very young, I remember being fascinated by tales of haunted houses and spirits of the past that roamed the darkened forests and roadsides during the dead of night just waiting for an unfortunate traveler to come along to hear their tragic stories. This interest stayed with me throughout the years and sharpened as I read every book I could find about famous haunted places far and wide. Soon, I found myself visiting some of these places to experience the history of the location and hopefully catch a glimpse of something paranormal, but I never *really* thought it was possible or could happen to me. However, that all changed on an August night in historic Jim Thorpe, Pennsylvania, back in 2001.

At the time, my fiancée (now my wife) and I were attending an introductory seminar on ghost hunting held by the Philadelphia Ghost Hunters Alliance at the Inn at Jim Thorpe. We were viewing the event only as a fun weekend getaway with the possibility of learning something new. To our delight, the seminar turned out to be extremely interesting and a great opportunity for training with some of the basic equipment and techniques used during paranormal investigations. On the second night of the event, we were very fortunate to have conducted a short investigation at the nearby gorgeous Asa Packer Mansion (built in 1861), guided by the attending members of the Philadelphia Ghost Hunter's Alliance. Here the employees of the estate educated us regarding the history of the lush mansion and the paranormal events experienced in the building throughout the years, which included everything imaginable up to sightings of full-bodied apparitions. They believed that the original owners of the mansion still walked the halls and kept watch over their beloved home from beyond the grave.

I soon realized that this could be a possibility while alone in a darkened bedroom on the third floor. I was using a night vision monocular to view the room when I was shocked to see a glowing orb the size of a baseball come out of a wall to my right at head level, pass directly in front of me and then vanish into another wall on the opposite side of the room. I initially thought it was a trick of some sort, or perhaps the headlights of a car from outside coming through the window. However, I then remembered that I was on the third floor, high above the ground surface. The heavy opaque drapes on the windows were drawn shut, and the room was in the rear right corner of the mansion and did not have a view of any nearby road. During the short time I observed the ball of light, I managed to close the eye I was using to look through the monocular and open my other eye to view the strange object without the aid of night vision. To my surprise, the orb was only visible while looking through the monocular. At the time, I remember feeling that I was not alone in the room and that this could be my first real encounter with a spiritual entity. Fortunately, I was not afraid, and the experience sent my mind reeling with possibilities and the desire to see more.

Later that night, I was with my fiancée, Olivia, and another couple in the first-floor study room taking pictures of the space in attempt to catch some photographic evidence of a spirit. I was so overwhelmed with the beauty of the building in general that I commented out loud regarding the exquisite craftsmanship of the woodwork with its detailed carvings. Playing on this, Olivia openly thanked the spirits in the house for letting us visit and experience the building. During this time, the two people with us were recording our investigation in this room with a digital audio recorder. When the night's investigation in the mansion was over, the four of us went back to our hotel room immediately to review the evidence. Upon listening to our audio recordings from the study room, we were floored to hear a response from an unidentified source on the device. After Olivia thanked the spirits for letting us visit the mansion, a grainy, but clear, disembodied voice answered with the phrase "You're welcome"! We knew that the voice did not belong to any of us, and we all agreed that we did not hear it at the time of the recording. To get a second opinion, we took the evidence to the lead investigator of the Philadelphia Ghost Hunter's Alliance for his analysis, and he exclaimed that the disembodied voice was indeed an electronic voice phenomenon (EVP) originating from a spirit. That specific EVP turned out to be the best sample of evidence collected by anyone attending the seminar that weekend and the starting point for my career in paranormal investigation. From that moment on, I was hooked and have been involved with paranormal investigations ever since.

It has been over ten years since my first brush with the paranormal, and since then I have conducted numerous paranormal investigations within my home state of Pennsylvania, as well as in other states, including New York, Arizona and West Virginia. In this field, I have worked on my own and as a member of paranormal research groups, where I have met and befriended interesting individuals such as local historians, psychic mediums and other paranormal researchers. Each location that I investigated provided me with new experiences and insight into the spiritual world. Initially for me, these investigations were more of a thrill-seeking hobby to see what sort of evidence I could collect. However, later on, this "hobby" evolved into a way to apply my knowledge of the physical sciences and engineering, further develop my spiritual growth, help frightened people living with spirit entities and potentially help the spirits themselves.

There are many possible reasons why a ghost of a deceased person would linger within the living world. Some more common explanations include the resolution of unfinished business, refusing to pass on because the spirit does not realize it is dead or simply choosing to stay behind at a certain location because the spirit loved it during life. As I stated previously, the latter could be the explanation of why the spirits of the Packers still remain in their past home. I learned that behind every true haunting there is an underlying history associated with it that is waiting to be discovered. By painstakingly unraveling the history, one could find the possible explanation for the haunting and the identity of the spirit involved with it. Once all the necessary details were uncovered about a haunting, then provisions could be made to help the residents of the location deal with the entity and help the spirit to pass on from the world of the living if that were the decided best course of action.

I believe ghosts should be treated with respect because, after all, they were once living persons with life experiences and memories. After my very first investigation at the Packer mansion, I discovered that utilizing aspects of a location's history during the investigation paired with treating the resident spirits with respect worked the best for me when it came time to review the evidence. For example, if we had not treated the Packers respectfully during our visit to the mansion and thanked them, I might not have witnessed that pivotal EVP that launched my career in paranormal investigations and essentially changed my life.

Years later, I now find myself to be the lead investigator and founder of the Scranton After Dark Paranormal Society (SADPS), a paranormal research group that investigates within the city of Scranton, Pennsylvania, and the surrounding areas. The SADPS works exclusively with the Lackawanna Historical Society (LHS) in an effort to raise funds for this important organization, which strives to keep the area's local history (even the darker side) alive for future generations to learn about and enjoy.

The tales of ghosts contained within the chapters of this book have originated from firsthand events experienced by the owners, employees, residents and/or patrons of the locations. These stories have been eagerly passed down throughout the years and survive to this day due to the general interest most people have regarding history, the afterlife and the paranormal. A large amount of the world's population today still believes in spirits and/or some form of the afterlife, and many of the living have had some unexplainable brushes with the supernatural, whether or not they will openly admit to it.

Modern science theorizes that energy can neither be truly created or destroyed but can be converted into another form of energy, such as electrical energy is converted to heat, mechanical or sound energy in common household appliances. What has been discovered through testing is that the energy conversion from one form to another is the most important aspect of this theory and that the before and after measurements of the converted energy surprisingly always total the same amount. I believe the same is true for the life energy of living creatures and that humans and animals are far more than just the bone, tissue and chemical energy that modern scientists claim them to be. Right now, we as humans do not comprehend or fully understand many aspects of the world we live in, let alone anything else beyond that, so it should not be hard to imagine the possibility that the life essence (energy) or "soul" of a living creature could still exist eternally after the body dies. This concept of life after death has existed in the majority of religions throughout the ages up until present times. If this energy is not truly destroyed as modern science suggests, it has to go somewhere, and this can be a plausible explanation for the existence of ghosts or spirits. From a much less scientific and religious point of view, the history portrayed in this book is a darker portion of local history. However, it is important that all history, good and bad, is preserved for the knowledge of future generations. From history, we can learn life lessons, find inspiration, appreciate aspects of life in past times and remember our mistakes and where we came from. In addition, the existence of and belief in ghosts can provide us with another possible link to this history.

I have taken great pleasure in researching the following locations within Scranton and providing the ghost lore and associated history in a written form for you readers to enjoy. However, this book is not intended to be a comprehensive guide to the history and/or haunted history of Scranton; rather, it is just a telling of the stories I know and have taken interest in. I have no doubt that there is enough similar additional information regarding Scranton to fill many more volumes. Before we begin our walk through some of the haunted history of Scranton, I would like to briefly introduce some relevant and important background information regarding the fine city where I was born and have worked for over thirteen years.

ONCE AN INDUSTRIAL EPICENTER

The Scranton, Pennsylvania, of today is a proud city born from the hard work and ingenuity of its first settlers. Scranton is affectionately referred to as the "Electric City" because it was the first city in the country to establish a successful pioneer electric trolley line back in 1886. However, in order to properly encompass the rich history of this city, we must regress back to a time even before this "electric" era and prior to any colonial settlement.

The Lackawanna Valley of the early 1700s consisted of a lush and dark wilderness populated by many species of large game animals, including deer, elk and even moose. Bear and mountain lion (cougar) stalked the forests and preyed on these animals, as did Native Americans. At this time, settlements of the Lenape, an Algonquin-speaking tribe, inhabited the valley, which provided them with rich soil for crops, good hunting and the waters of the Lackawanna River for drinking, bathing, fishing and transportation. In fact, Lackawanna is derived from *Lech-uh-wanna*, an old Lenni-Lenape word meaning "stream that forks." The specific area of the valley that encompassed today's city of Scranton was occupied in the mid-1700s by the Munsee tribe of Native Americans and was then called Capoose Meadows after the chief of the tribe, Capoose, who was noted for his knowledge of agriculture and peaceful ways.

Eventually, this fertile and flourishing valley was settled in the late 1700s by Europeans, who were drawn to the area for much the same reasons as the natives. These people were of English descent and migrated into northeastern Pennsylvania from parts of New England to harvest timber and farm the fertile virgin land of the Lackawanna Valley. For a time, the settlers lived in peace with the Munsee tribe, who gradually migrated westward into the Ohio Valley after granting their claimed lands to be sold to the white settlers in 1743, the majority of which were later purchased by Governor Penn in 1758. In the 1770s, the Tripp and Slocum families were among the first of the white settlers to the region. Isaac Tripp built a home in 1771 in what is now the Providence section of the city, and the Slocums established a farm near the location of today's Scranton south side area, which later became a small village named Slocum Hollow.

During that period, there were many heated disputes regarding land acquisitions for the area between the colonial Connecticut claims of land granted by the king of England and the newer claims of the colonial government of Pennsylvania. Daily life for the settlers became a dangerous fight for survival during the American Revolution because the British army often controlled and provoked attacks on their settlements with groups of Native Americans. At the direction of the British, Isaac Tripp himself was shot and killed in 1779 by natives in the area of nearby Wilkes-Barre, Pennsylvania. The settlers of the Lackawanna Valley and neighboring Wyoming Valley had to be on guard at all times for attacks and kept weapons close at hand while tending to their crops. On July 3, 1778, a contingent of approximately 300 American militiamen faced an onslaught of a much larger force of British soldiers, Tories and natives near modern-day Exeter, which lies approximately twelve miles south of Scranton. A frenzy and massacre ensued when thousands of settlers fled in panic for their lives as the invaders killed many civilians and destroyed their homes, crops and livestock. The American forts in the area were surrendered or abandoned as the British army's wake of destruction extended up into the Lackawanna Valley. This attack will be forever known in the annals of history as the "Battle of Wyoming" and the "Wyoming

Massacre." This tumultuous period for the settlers came to an end in 1779, when a contingent of 2,500 American soldiers led by General John Sullivan marched through the area and crippled the villages of the natives who were assisting the British army and drove them out of the valley forever.

In 1838, George and Selden Scranton moved to the region, purchased the old Slocum property and constructed an iron-manufacturing plant that was fueled by the plentiful anthracite (coal) obtained from local mining operations. The mining of coal forever changed the face of the area as the Lackawanna Iron and Coal Company was formed and became the first successful business in the United States to mass produce "T" rails for the railroads, which developed into the lifeline of the region and country. Scranton became the major rail-manufacturing city in the United States by 1856, the year it was incorporated into a borough. In 1851, the Scrantons formed the Delaware, Lackawanna and Western Railroad (DL&W) as a means to transport iron and coal goods from the Lackawanna Valley to the rest of the United States.

Scranton was incorporated as a city on April 23, 1866, and soon evolved into an urban and industrial center as a result of the expansion of the country's railroads and the success of its coal and iron businesses. By the turn of the century, the city of Scranton was home to five major railroads, and over 80 percent of the world's known anthracite reserves were located in northeastern Pennsylvania, with Scranton at its heart. The coal from this region spurred the industrial development of the country and lasted as the primary source of heating for homes in the eastern states for some seventy-five years.

At its high point in the early 1900s, Scranton received a massive influx of people of all sorts who brought their own individual talents and ingenuity to assist with the growth and development of the city. A vast number of immigrants came to find work associated with the local industries, such as coal mining, iron and steel manufacturing, the railroads and textile manufacturing. In addition, many wealthy businessmen and entrepreneurs were attracted by the possibility of developing successful businesses in a quickly growing region. Soon afterward, Scranton evolved into one of the country's premier cities and

A panoramic view of late 1800s downtown Scranton, Pennsylvania, at the end of the nineteenth century. *Courtesy of the Lackawanna Historical Society.*

spurred many technological and civic innovations for the local region and the rest of the nation. At that time, Scranton also boasted some of the nation's most architecturally beautiful buildings as a trademark to its success. These elaborate structures were designed by some of the most prominent architects of the time, including Raymond Hood (Cultural Center), Kenneth Murchison (Lackawanna Station) and Isaac Perry (courthouse), and still stand today providing a tangible window into this past era.

At one time for the region coal was king, but it is common knowledge that no era, good or bad, lasts forever. The city of Scranton reached its peak in population in 1930, at over 143,000, and since has steadily declined to around 76,000, mostly due to changes within industry and economy as the nation developed. Even though Scranton is not the booming metropolis of its heyday, the city and surrounding region still remain as a good place to live and raise a family due to their inexpensive cost of living and ever-increasing quality of life. In addition, the hardworking locals who remain here still possess the rich culture of their family heritages and provide the area with its own unique small hometown feel and pride—a feeling that is not present everywhere in this country and I believe is declining due to today's fast-paced modern ways of living.

Despite the inevitable changes to the world and to the ways of life over time, the unseen ghosts of the past are still lingering everywhere not far out of reach to remind us of what dwelt here before. Around every turn, in darkness or in light, there is always a chance to stumble into one of these harbingers of history when you least expect it. Be prepared, for the next time you feel a sudden unexplained cold draft on the back of your neck or hear creaking on the staircase when no one is there, it may be just the wind or the building settling. However, it also could be the spirits of the past trying to get your attention.

1

THE CATLIN HOUSE

DID THE CATLINS EVER LEAVE?

At 232 Monroe Avenue, within the heart of the University of Scranton campus, sits an exquisitely preserved and beautifully decorated slice of local history. This stately three-story antique gem of a building presently stands enveloped by the looming modernized university—offices, lecture halls and recreation centers—like a hidden treasure waiting to be discovered. The home is presently one of the few remaining estates in that area of the city that formerly consisted of a neighborhood containing the most prominent and important names in the region, such as Scranton and Archbald. This picturesque structure with its peaked roofs and striped awnings was designed by the architect Edward Langley in the English Tudor Revival style and constructed in 1912 as the private sixteen-room home of the once successful Scranton lawyer and banker George Catlin and his second wife, Helen.

George Catlin was born on August 26, 1845, in Shoreham, Vermont, to Lynde Catlin and Amelia Harriet Moore. He graduated from Union College in 1866 with an undergraduate degree in law but soon afterward, in 1867, received a master's degree from Lafayette College. George was then admitted to the New York state bar in Albany and later worked for the law firm of Pope, Thompson and

Catlin at 17 Nassau Street in New York City. He married his first wife, Mary Woodrow Archbald, in the same year he joined the law firm, and the couple lived in New York City for several years before relocating to Scranton, Pennsylvania, in 1870 for unknown reasons. George may have been enticed into moving to Scranton because it was a fairly new and rapidly growing city where one had great potential to become successful and make a name for himself by his own ingenuity. Perhaps for this reason, soon after reaching Scranton, George decided to end his short-stemmed law career to pursue the matter of finances. This new endeavor may have been influenced by the economic boom occurring in Scranton at this time due to the start of some very successful coal-mining and iron-manufacturing businesses that were generating great sums of money and prompted the need for local banks. However, the couple may have simply relocated to Scranton

The former home of George and Helen Catlin at 232 Monroe Avenue. It is now the headquarters of the Lackawanna Historical Society (LHS). *Courtesy of the Lackawanna Historical Society.*

because his wife had family in the city, with whom the Catlins decided to make their home after arriving.

In 1872, George Catlin became the organizer and founder of the Third National Bank in Scranton. He served as vice-president for a number of years and as director for an astounding sixty-three years up until the time of his death. The ambitious Mr. Catlin also served as director of the Scranton Savings Bank, the Scranton Street Railway Company, the Erie & Wyoming Valley Railroad and the Crown Point Iron Company. However, George's ambition and passion also was channeled into other interests, such as the importance of preserving local history. This interest eventually prompted him to join the Lackawanna Institute of History and Science in 1886. The group's main focus was to preserve the local history of Lackawanna County, which is the youngest in the state. Mary Archbald Catlin passed away in 1902, and George was remarried on January 10, 1904, to Helen Walsh of Carbondale, Pennsylvania. The new couple built their home at 232 Monroe Avenue in 1912, which still stands today in its full splendor. Throughout the years they spent within the home, the Catlins held regular events. They even had some servants, but unfortunately neither marriage provided any offspring for George Catlin. However, the Catlins did have many nieces and nephews who visited and stayed with them often.

The Lackawanna Institute of History and Science later became known as the Lackawanna Historical Society (LHS) in 1921 and was designated as the official historical society of Lackawanna County in 1965. George Catlin died in his home on June 8, 1935, after suffering a short illness at the age of ninety. Interestingly enough, his will directed that the Catlin family home be given to the Lackawanna Historical Society, along with all its interior furnishings and belongings, upon the death of his wife so that it could benefit the people of Scranton and permanently be known as the George H. Catlin Memorial. Mrs. Helen Catlin died in 1942 after suffering a long illness at the home of her sister. Her former house at 232 Monroe Avenue was bequeathed to the LHS in that year and has served as the organization's headquarters since that time. In the following years, the George H. Catlin Memorial

George and Helen Catlin relaxing by the water. *Courtesy of the Lackawanna Historical Society.*

has remained true to its original purpose and the wish of George Catlin to serve as a cultural center for the people of the city. Today, the staff and volunteers of the Catlin House accommodate exhibits, lectures, events and research activities with the focus of educating people of all ages about the history of Lackawanna County and keeping that history alive for generations to come. The LHS is not only a valuable source of historical information and references for the entire local community, but the building itself also serves as a literal window to the past and contains countless artifacts, relics, books, photographs and other documents from Pennsylvania's history that date back as far as the 1700s. The majority of these artifacts were once the personal belongings of the Catlins and others from the area or are linked to important historical events such as the Civil War.

One possible reason for the paranormal activity experienced in the building may be the result of spirit connection to some of the hundreds of historical artifacts contained here. This phenomenon is believed to occur when an artifact holds a particularly strong and profound significance to a person in life and his or her spirit becomes linked to it in death. The artifact could be anything ranging from a beloved personal belonging, such as a wedding ring or an entire home, to a military-issued rifle that a soldier used during combat in a bloody historic battle. Recent stories regarding spirit connection throughout the world have suggested that it can also exist with some strange items, including a bed that a specific person died in or a brick from a dismantled church that was used in the construction of a new apartment building. In the years following that particular person's death, the spirit-linked item may be relocated or become the property of someone else. At this time, the new owners and/or others close to them can experience evidence of a haunting resulting from the spirit of the item's original possessor.

In recent years, the Catlin House has been known to be active with spiritual energy and host to a number of strange and possibly supernatural occurrences. The recent reported paranormal encounters experienced by the members of the Lackawanna Historical Society (LHS) staff and volunteers within the building include everything from uneasy feelings to sightings of full-bodied apparitions. These encounters have been experienced throughout the entire building, from the basement to the third floor. Many LHS workers and volunteers have reported some apprehension about descending into the bowels of the basement when the need arises to obtain some extra chairs for an event upstairs or something else along those lines. This feeling is not so uncommon with people in general, since most do not welcome being underground in a dimly lit and damp enclosed space with few windows to the outside. These conditions, combined with an overactive imagination, can often make the mind mistakenly see things that are not really there—such as shadows moving in one's peripheral vision. Add in the suggestion of a haunting and people could formulate false explanations for mundane noises within the building that have very rational and non-paranormal sources. Suddenly, the creaking of the house settling becomes disembodied footsteps on the wooden staircase as the individual experiencing the sound becomes increasingly more frightened.

These explanations could simply be the case with the basement of the old Catlin House, or it could be something entirely more mysterious. In this space, people often feel sudden drafts or cold spots that appear and vanish without warning or explanation, hear disembodied voices, experience feelings of dread and sense unseen eyes on them. While visiting the basement, people sensitive to spirits have also explained that the presence of the workers who constructed the house still lingers down there, but there is really no definitive reason why. For example, there were no tragic accidents documented or known to have occurred during the construction of the house, and no one is believed to be buried beneath the foundation. Perhaps the original builders took so much pride in the construction of this masterpiece that a part of them has been written into the very wood and stone of the structure.

In addition, workers and visitors in the building often report a "heaviness" on the second floor, where the old servants' quarters once existed. This area now houses a small office and rooms that contain costumes and mannequins for the exhibits displayed throughout the old home. However, it is still evident today that the furnishings and design of the rooms in the servants' area of the house are far less grand than where the members of the actual Catlin family spent their time, and by stepping through the threshold into this area, one can literally feel the distinct separation. These were the rooms where the house servants to the Catlin family performed some of their duties. The strange aura here could possibly represent a residual uneasiness or tension between employee and employer that remains to the present day.

Similarly, an adjacent room on the second floor, called the "fashion room" since it contains numerous displays of some antique dresses and clothing, has also been a hot spot in the building for uncomfortable feelings, which seem to be oddly centered within a large closet located in the room. While placing boxes in the closet, one volunteer had the sudden feeling that he was not alone in the room. The man was on his hands and knees at the time, carefully sliding boxes into the bottom shelves of the closet below numerous hanging garments. He turned around to look behind him and saw no one there, so he simply shrugged off the feeling and quietly returned to his work. After several moments, the man could sense the eyes of someone watching him again. However, this time he did not have to turn around because he felt that whoever was responsible was inside the closet with him. Sure enough, and to his utter shock, the man's gaze was directed upward, and he saw that one of the antique gowns hanging nearby suddenly appeared as though it were filled out by the form of a body without legs or feet. The volunteer was so scared that he ran out of the room without finishing his work or staying to find out who—or what—was wearing the gown.

While organizing articles of clothing within this same closet sometime later, a female volunteer was overcome by the feeling that she had actually been transported back in time for several moments. She recalled hearing the whistle of a steam locomotive engine while she was working in the closet and was literally surrounded by tangible bits of history. This type of phenomenon is known as a warp or vortex in the field of the paranormal and is not uncommon at haunted locations that have, or have experienced, a great deal of history. Within a warp or vortex, the fabric of the past and present can overlap for a short period of time, and those individuals caught inside it will see the location as it was years or sometimes centuries before. There is a famous story from Gettysburg, Pennsylvania, that originated in the 1980s and regards the oldest building on the Gettysburg College campus, Pennsylvania Hall, which was utilized as a makeshift hospital for wounded soldiers during the Battle of Gettysburg in July 1863. One night, while working late in the building, two administrators meant to take the elevator from their upper-floor offices to the exit on the first floor, but instead the elevator doors opened in the basement, which was used for storage. Instead of finding a dark storage room devoid of life, the men were shocked to see a full-fledged Civil War hospital, complete with doctors, orderlies and patients. The two frightened men never left the elevator and pounded frantically on the buttons to escape the horrifying scene. Suddenly, the elevator doors closed and took them to the first floor, where they exited and ran to find a security guard, to whom they explained the horrific event. The administrators returned to the basement of the building several minutes later with the security guard and were very surprised and embarrassed to see it was empty, with the exception of items stored there by the college.

Some of the staff members and volunteers strongly believe that the Catlin family and possibly their servants may have never left the beloved home, and their spiritual presence is still rooted within the building. This belief can be taken quite seriously when the strange experiences in the house are taken into consideration. One LHS member and volunteer related a chilling event that occurred several years ago during the annual LHS Holiday Open House. During this Christmas-inspired event, the Catlin House is beautifully decorated in traditional holiday fashion and boasts time-honored holiday fare, along with live entertainment for all the guests. It is a two-day event that hosts the LHS members and volunteers exclusively on the first night and is open to the public on the second evening. On the members-only night that particular year, one woman who openly admitted to being sensitive to spirits witnessed something shocking and unexpected. She was sitting at a table in the rear room on the first floor, which serves as the working office for LHS staff workers. The woman was intensely engaged in conversation with a few friends and fellow LHS volunteers also sitting at the table and was facing the rear entrance door to the house when something odd caught her attention. Two women clothed in elaborate early 1900s period gowns suddenly appeared near the rear doorway within her line of sight. These figures walked right past the table where she was sitting through a short corridor and vanished into a closed door, beyond which leads straight into the library room for the historical references used by the LHS. The woman remarked that she did not remember hearing the door to the outside open before the figures appeared and also did not feel the cold draft of air that would have occurred when the winter air wafted in following the opening of the door. Stranger still was the fact that the closed door through which the figures stepped is totally blocked on the other side by a bookcase in the library room. Although no one else present witnessed the event, which lasted only several seconds, the woman was convinced that she had seen a pair of ghosts that were tied to the history of the old home. Perhaps some of the original Catlin family decided to attend the holiday party as well that year.

Another LHS volunteer related a strange event that occurred in the second-floor bathroom and is immediately adjacent to the fashion room closet that was previously mentioned. This bathroom is decorated to look as it did when the Catlin family was living in the home and is not presently operational. This room is used only as a historical exhibit and contains a female mannequin dressed in period bedtime clothing, which is strangely involved with the encounter. While visiting the second floor of the house, a female volunteer passed by the small bathroom and suddenly felt as though someone were looking at her from inside that room. She halted in mid-stride and reluctantly peered into the bathroom, hoping that it was just her imagination. The woman was chilled to the bone when the mannequin's head appeared to rise slowly, as if to look at her. Needless to say, the volunteer screamed and ran out of the building.

To this day, she is convinced that the mannequin moved on its own and that the event was not merely her imagination or an optical illusion.

Who knows, the mannequin may have been momentarily animated by the spirit of a former Catlin servant to let her know that they are still present in the house and going about their daily routines. In reality, that possibility certainly exists considering the amount of use the building has endured during the one hundred years since it was constructed and the large amount of history contained within.

2

THE LACKAWANNA STATION HOTEL

TERROR ON THE SIXTH FLOOR

The success of the Lackawanna Iron and Coal Company founded by George and Selden Scranton in the mid-1800s was pivotal to the expansion of the Lackawanna Valley and the rest of the county due to its production of iron—and later, steel—"T" rails, which were used to construct the railroads. This initial venture, paired with the realization that railroads would be key to the industrial growth of the area, eventually spurned George Scranton to construct the Leggett's Gap Railroad, which was later merged with the Delaware and Cobbs Gap Railroad to establish the Delaware, Lackawanna and Western Railroad Company (DL&W). The DL&W was the first railroad to pass through the area that was to become known as Scranton and soon became the region's lifeline by supplying the rest of the country with iron and coal goods. By the early 1900s, the booming city of Scranton was host to five major railroads that transported goods and passengers all over the United States. As a result, the need for an adequately sized train station in the city developed and was answered by the construction of the building currently located at 700 Lackawanna Avenue, which formerly served as the DL&W Railroad passenger terminal in Scranton. The new station was constructed to replace a smaller one that was originally located about seven blocks westward, near the present-day corner of Lackawanna and Franklin Avenues.

This gorgeous six-story structure was erected in 1908 and designed in the Beaux Arts style of the French Renaissance by a renowned New York City architect named Kenneth Murchison in 1906. The station took only fourteen months to complete and cost $600,000 to build. It is constructed out of brick and steel, with concrete floors and partitions. The building's exterior is faced with Indiana limestone and the façade contains an eight-foot-diameter bronze clock set between detailed carvings of two enormous eagles. The interior of the building is no less elegant and beautiful, containing furnishings of imported marble and a barrel-vaulted ceiling made of stained glass. The structure was originally only five stories tall, the sixth floor being added in the 1920s to provide for additional office space. In later years, the railroads were gradually replaced by other forms of transportation such as cars, buses and airplanes. The station eventually fell into disuse and was closed in January 1970. However, in December 1977, costly renovations of the building began and continued until 1983, when it reopened as a hotel, and in 1995, it became the Radisson Lackawanna Station Hotel. Despite the extensive restoration and conversion of the building's use, special care was taken to ensure that the existing features—such as clocks, doors, fountains, staircases, walls and ceilings—were preserved and retained their original overall appearance. However, time and careful restoration does not always erase all blemishes and unwanted features, especially the ones that can't be seen and are hiding just beneath the surface—like ghosts.

Up until very recently, the Radisson Lackawanna Station Hotel was very tight-lipped about the presence of any paranormal activity within the building. In the past, management did not want the building to have the notoriety for being haunted; perhaps for fear that it might detract from the current ambiance of the building or attract a large number of unintended types of guests, such as ghost hunters and thrill-seekers. However, possibly due to the current popularity of ghosts and hauntings in the media, management is now open enough about the subject to allow its inclusion in newspaper articles, books and even the local historic ghost-

The Lackawanna Station shortly after the construction, circa 1908. *Courtesy of the Lackawanna Historical Society.*

walking tour, called "Scranton After Dark," put on by the Lackawanna Historical Society. Nevertheless, it was a secret that could not have stayed hidden forever and suggests that the present-day hotel is host to a number of resident spirits that seemingly never checked out.

The basement of the building was used during World War I as a morgue for slain soldiers whose bodies were in transit to their final resting places. The particular section of the basement once used for this purpose is said to be the haunting ground for the spirit of a young boy wearing a top hat. Several staff members and visitors have seen this boy on occasion, but no one really knows who he is, and it is strange because the boy is too young to be a World War I soldier. However, it is possible that this boy's body was also being transported back to his hometown on a train and was temporarily stored in the basement. Perhaps his spirit had some final business or missed the chance to pass on from the world of the living and stayed with his body until reaching the station, where it chose to remain forever.

The rail yards behind the station (center) and the covered boarding platform at the Lackawanna Station (far right-hand side of the photograph). This is where travelers would exit the cars and proceed into the station. *Courtesy of the Lackawanna Historical Society.*

As strange as the basement of the building may seem, it contains only a small portion of the reported paranormal activity in the hotel. Guests staying at the hotel have witnessed strange occurrences on the upper floors of the structure as well, with the sixth being the most active. While staying on this floor, some guests have admitted to receiving a sudden and unexpected knock on their door from an African American bellhop. The man asked them if everything was OK and then vanished into thin air right before their eyes. He may have been a previous employee who is still making his rounds in the hotel. In addition, numerous other guests staying on the floor have reported light switches turning off and on repeatedly by themselves, along with experiences of extreme and sudden changes in temperature, usually freezing cold, with no apparent cause.

The most well known of these tales involves a group of minor-league baseball players who were in town for a series of games against the local Scranton/Wilkes-Barre team in 2006. One of the players reported waking up during the night at 2:00 a.m. to a freezing cold room and could not move. He felt as though he were being pinned down by an unseen force for about twenty to thirty seconds and could not struggle to free himself. Upon being released, he immediately turned on the lights, looked into the bathroom mirror and saw what appeared to be red claw marks on both of his forearms and biceps. The man was so frightened that he sat awake until his roommate returned from a night out at the local bars. On the same trip, one evening at about midnight, several of the teammates were walking the hallway of the sixth floor when they encountered a man who was leaning over a railing six floors above the dining room. The man turned to face the players and told them that he was killed in a car accident. Then the group was horrified to witness the man's head spin around a full 360 degrees and watched him fall over the railing, only to disappear in mid-flight. This story is incredible and nearly unbelievable; however, the players involved were not drinking alcohol at the time and insisted that they were telling the truth. On another trip, two other baseball roommates had a strange encounter with a light switch while staying in one of the sixth-floor guest rooms. One

The lavish and elegant interior lobby of the Lackawanna Station. *Courtesy of the Lackawanna Historical Society.*

of the players was in the bathroom using the sink when the lights unexpectedly turned off. The man turned the light switch back on, only to witness it flip to the off position by itself. He was confused and a little shocked, so he called to his roommate and explained what had happened. The other player then forcefully switched the lights back on, and both men were shocked to see the switch flip off and on rapidly by itself for about ten seconds. They felt that something paranormal had occurred, and they had heard about similar stories of the hotel from other players, so they ran down to the front desk to change rooms.

It might be easy to suggest that the above stories of the players are just mere baseball folklore meant to frighten other players staying at the hotel. However, even though the current staff is reluctant to divulge any information about ghosts, a few former employees of the hotel have revealed that they believe the sixth floor is indeed haunted, and similar events have been witnessed by other guests staying at the hotel who were not minor-league baseball players. One member and volunteer of the Lackawanna Historical Society related a tale about his own strange experiences while staying at the hotel several years ago. The man attended a high school reunion at the hotel and was staying overnight in one of the guest rooms. He remembered waking up late in the night to a freezing cold room, but he fell back asleep, and nothing else out of the ordinary seemed to occur at that time. However, when he awoke in the morning and was in the bathroom washing his face, he realized that he had quite a prominent black eye. The man stated that he did not fall or bump his face on anything the night before at the reunion and certainly had not been struck by another one of the guests. Being familiar with the history and lore of the building, he suggested that he might have been attacked by a spirit in his room while he was sleeping. However, the black eye could have been the result of a blood vessel near his eye rupturing on its own.

The Radisson Lackawanna Station Hotel is certainly a beautiful, historic and interesting building. The reasons for the paranormal activity experienced within its walls are not currently explained, and the only known suspicious death in the building occurred during the major

The beautiful Tiffany glass ceiling inside the Lackawanna Station. Note the railing, over which the spirit of the man was said to have fallen. *Courtesy of the Lackawanna Historical Society.*

renovation in the late 1970s. The local police reported that a deceased homeless man was found in the building; he had likely sneaked in at night through one of the construction openings and died inside. However, thousands of people have passed through its doors due to its initial use as a train station and, more recently, as a hotel, and any building or location that has seen that many people over a long period of time is likely to have some ghost lore associated with it.

3

COURTHOUSE SQUARE

THE LADY IN WHITE AND OTHER MACABRE TALES

At the true heart of the city are Courthouse Square and its surrounding grounds, which were totally redesigned and refurbished several years ago during a multimillion-dollar renovation. Today, there are monuments on the square to honor the likes of George Washington, Christopher Columbus, Phil Sheridan, Casimir Pulaski, John Mitchell, Thaddeus Kosciuszko, local Medal of Honor recipients and actor Jason Miller, among others. The striking and immense Soldiers' and Sailors' Monument along North Washington Avenue honors Civil War veterans. The square grounds might now have a truly modern twenty-first-century appearance, but the original courthouse building, which was designed by architect Isaac Perry, still stands proudly at its center as it has since 1884, six years after Lackawanna County was incorporated. The land that the square and the Lackawanna County Courthouse building now occupy was originally a natural wetland named Lily Pond, which was donated by the Lackawanna Iron and Coal Company and the Susquehanna and Wyoming Valley Railroad Company. Prior to construction, the swamp was filled in with slag waste material from the nearby ironworks to make a level pad area for the erection of the building and development of the grounds. It should be noted that one would be very hard pressed to get such a project to develop a natural wetland through the environmental permitting process today.

An original sketch of Lily Pond as it appeared prior to the construction of the Lackawanna Courthouse Building and Courthouse Square. *Courtesy of the Lackawanna Historical Society.*

However, the chosen location turned out to be an ideal area for the square and courthouse building and helped to establish a more central downtown location for the city. The nearby area along Penn Avenue had previously served as the main business center for Scranton, but the county commissioners aimed to continue city growth by opening this new area to development. Courthouse Square was designed similarly to most American city squares, with important civic buildings located at the center and other public and commercial buildings around the perimeter. The surrounding grounds provided an open green space, which created a tranquil park-like setting in the center of the bustling city for the public and served to establish a focal point in the growing community. In the early 1900s, the square offered an ideal area for shoppers to rest and where picnics and concert events could be held. As the downtown area flourished, the need for convenient public restrooms arose and soon prompted the construction of an underground comfort station located beneath Courthouse Square.

This comfort station was a true masterpiece of engineering designed by a local architect named Frederick A. Fletcher. The impressive structure had poured concrete walls eighteen inches thick, measuring eighteen feet in width by sixty-four feet in length, to guard against dampness. In addition, the floor of the comfort station was located twelve feet beneath the ground surface. The station was the first of its kind outside the larger cities of the time like Philadelphia, Washington, D.C., and Boston and contained separate restroom entrances for men and women at opposite ends of the structure. A special circulation system conducted a complete air exchange approximately every three minutes and passed fresh air over coils for heat in the winter and provided cool air conditioning in the summer. The structure was invisible from the surface, with the exception of the surface vents and entrances. Inside the buried outer walls, the station contained five interior rooms, which were composed of materials such as marble, white enamel and brass. They looked elegant but were installed largely for their ease with sanitation. The rooms were even constructed to be rounded off so that dirt, grim and debris could be easily swept away and would not collect in the corners. The installation of the innovative comfort station certainly provided some added convenience and luxury to the rapidly developing downtown area. Unfortunately, many years later, the comfort station fell into disuse and became a haven for criminals, vagrants and the like. The city eventually removed the entrances and filled in the structure with earth, thus eliminating a growing liability.

As with any city or location where human beings gather in larger amounts, there is always the ever-lingering presence of the lawless or self-governed members of society who commit both impulsive and premeditated acts of crime. During the city's heyday, Scranton was no exception to this rule and hosted more than its share of resident

An original rendering of the Lackawanna County Courthouse building by architect Isaac Perry. *Courtesy of the Lackawanna Historical Society.*

and nomadic murderers. These people were responsible for the most heinous of crimes in the city, such as the following documented events, which will be forever etched into the history and lore of downtown Scranton.

One evening in November 1932, the unthinkable happened. Freshly released from a prison in Auburn, New York, a man named Joseph Kosh was in Scranton and met the owner of a notorious local brothel. Her true name was Victoria Smolinsky, but she worked under the alias Marie King. The two seemingly hit it off and had Thanksgiving dinner together. However, she refused his advances to spend the night, possibly because he did not possess the funds to compensate her. The next morning, Joseph unexpectedly showed up at her home with a fifteen-inch-long bread knife he had stolen from a local lunchroom and cornered her. Her friends present in the house at the time heard her plead for her life, but the man savagely stabbed her twenty times with the knife before he could be stopped and arrested. The local police later called Joseph the most dangerous and unruly prisoner they had ever handled. While imprisoned, he attempted to take his own life repeatedly by hanging, stabbing and burning himself. He is reported to have said the following about the crime: "I gave Marie King the works because she tried to double cross me; when she cried for mercy, I only laughed."

Joseph Kosh later received his wish for death when he was executed for his despicable crime. The former address of Ms. King's brothel and home was 231 Raymond Court, which is near the present-day location of 126 Franklin Avenue (formerly Whistle's Pub). On a lighter note, the memorial statue of Christopher Columbus (mentioned previously), which stands on the square at the corner of North Washington Avenue and Spruce Street, triumphantly points in this direction. There is a saying among Scranton natives today that if you want to know where the red-light district once existed in the city, simply follow in the direction pointed by this monument.

On May 5, 1924, a criminal named John Myma, alias Frank Dugan, entered a jewelry and pawn shop owned by a man named Wolf Glou located along Lackawanna Avenue near what would be the Marquee Cinema today. Myma pawned a watch at the shop but was displeased with the price he received for it. He reluctantly took the money and left the store in an uproar. In a fit of rage, Myma stormed across the road to the railroad tracks and found a fourteen-inch-long steel bar with a nut attached to one end. Myma later returned to Wolf Glou's shop, savagely beat the shopkeeper with the steel bar and robbed the store. However, the shopkeeper's son-in-law heard the commotion and soon appeared on the scene. He pursued the criminal as he fled the shop, caught up with him and tackled and restrained him until the police could arrive and arrest the thief. Unfortunately, Wolf Glou died from the injuries received in the beating. John Myma was later tried and executed for his impulsive act of murder.

Unfortunately, criminal acts such as this were as common back then as they are today, and in the days when Lackawanna County was young, execution by hanging was used as a final punishment for those who committed the worst of crimes. In the late 1800s and early 1900s, several local men who committed murder in Lackawanna County were indeed hanged for their crimes, and these executions took place at the county seat in Scranton. The very first of these hangings were public events carried out at the gallows previously located outside on Courthouse Square. No physical evidence of the gallows can be seen in the now-modernized and picturesque square, but this archaic implement of execution is believed to have been located in the vicinity of the present-day John Mitchell memorial statue, which stands behind the courthouse building on Adams Avenue.

It is known that most of these criminals did not meet their sentences calmly and often defiantly fought back against their captors, spewing forth taunts and curses until the bitter and sudden end of their lives at the end of a rope. In addition, at least one of them was strangled to death by the noose after hanging for over twenty minutes because his neck did not break during the initial drop. Spectacles like this were controversial and not really fit for public consumption, especially in a city that was then booming with business and industry and rapidly becoming distinctly cosmopolitan. Because of this, the executions were later moved into a private room in the jail on North Washington Avenue and out of the public eye forever. By the early 1920s, execution by hanging in Pennsylvania had been replaced with electrocution in the electric chair. The fierce emotions of these sentenced men and the stress of their executions could have very well set the stage for future hauntings or left residual imprints of the events. After death, their restless spirits might have decided to remain and tend to unfinished business or seek revenge on the ones who sentenced them. Another possibility is that the events that transpired in their lives so long ago and ultimately led up to their executions rendered them unable to pass on and left their souls stranded on Courthouse Square to this very day. Perhaps this is why the Lackawanna Courthouse building is publicly known as a haunted location today.

A photograph of the original Lackawanna Courthouse building and surrounding grounds in downtown Scranton, Pennsylvania. *Courtesy of the Lackawanna Historical Society.*

The once nearby public executions and the emotional court trials within the building since 1884 may indeed be a few of the likely explanations for the ghost sightings and paranormal experiences of numerous people ranging from janitors to judges in the courthouse building throughout the years. Nighttime workers in the building have frequently reported experiencing lights turning off or back on again by themselves in rooms that were locked and had no one in them at the time. This is known to happen most often in the old marriage license office on the third floor for some unknown reason. The event always baffles the sheriffs working late in the building and gives them an uneasy feeling that they are not alone. Workers also often hear footsteps in empty hallways and feel very cold gusts of air that appear suddenly and without warning on warm nights and have no seemingly logical source. Another notorious area of the building for uneasy feelings is the bell tower, where sheriffs have reluctantly admitted that they do not wish to go due to seeing moving shadows and feeling as though they are being watched.

Some other workers in the building have had much more memorable experiences with the resident spirits of the courthouse. Such was the case with a member of the cleaning crew who came face to face with the building's most infamous spirit, "the lady in white," one night about ten years ago in the darkened second-floor hallway. Interestingly enough, ghostly tales regarding a "white lady" have also originated in many parts of the United States and all over the world, for that matter. This type of female spirit is most often associated with some local legend involving a great tragedy, such as a sudden and horrific death at a key moment in life, betrayal or the loss of a child or husband. For example, in Altoona, Pennsylvania, there is a legend about the White Lady of Whopsy, who haunts Whopsononock and Buckhorn Mountain along a dangerous stretch of road called the Devil's Elbow, where it is said that she and her husband died in a terrible crash many years ago. Her spirit is sometimes seen on foggy nights walking along the side of the road, still looking for her husband. She has been known to hitch a ride from people driving the road, only to vanish into thin air when the site of the crash is reached. Similar legends of a white lady also exist in New Jersey, New York, Connecticut, Washington, Florida, England, Germany, Portugal, Norway, Brazil and other locations.

In the case of the Lackawanna County Courthouse, nobody seems to know who she is or why the spirit is present in the building. The maintenance worker who sighted her explained that he was finished with his shift and was about to leave for the night when he realized that he had left some personal belongings on the second floor. No one else was around, and the place was quiet when he returned to the second floor. The unfortunate man was scared senseless by what he saw in the hallway heading toward him. He had heard the tales about the lady in white from his co-workers, who had been employed in the building for many years, but he had never dreamed he would run into the legendary spirit face to face. To his sheer horror, the ghostly white semitransparent figure of a woman floating in mid-air slowly drifted toward him. He tried to run but was frozen in place at the sight of the unearthly spirit, which just sailed silently right over his head without seeming to acknowledge his presence. This spirit has been sighted in a similar fashion from time to time by other workers on the second floor throughout the years. In addition to her, a lone transparent male figure, as well as a ghostly couple, has been witnessed on the first floor of the building in recent years.

However, paranormal encounters on the square are by no means limited to the courthouse building and grounds. Odd experiences have also been reported in a building across the street from the courthouse, at 205 North Washington Avenue, on the two floors above where the Subway restaurant is located. Currently, the upper levels house several local law offices, where some of the employees have admitted to the presence of ghostly activity. One lawyer in particular who had his interest in the supernatural sparked while working alone in the building at night reported often hearing shuffling or footsteps echoing down the hallway past his office room after hours when he had seen everyone leave for the day and had locked the front door. Thinking that someone had broken into building, the lawyer would leave his workstation to investigate and find no one there. This would happen on such a frequent basis that he just learned to expect it while working late. In addition, he and other employees also experienced isolated roving cold spots and the sound of keys jingling nearby when no one else was around. Perhaps these encounters are the result of a long-deceased janitor who is still performing his nightly cleaning duties in the building.

Although it is located about one mile from the center of the city, the Lackawanna County Jail is tied to Courthouse Square in history since it is where many of the criminals who were sentenced to incarceration in Lackawanna County later spent some time. The prison was originally built in the 1880s to detain 110 prisoners but was expanded in 1999 to hold a maximum of 1,200 male and female inmates. Interestingly enough, the newer portion of the jail was built over an older burial site. Today, the facility provides all of the necessary services to the inmates from food, medical treatment and recreation to computer training, counseling and rehabilitation programs. However, even with all the provided "amenities," prison is undoubtedly a very difficult situation for most people to endure, to say the least. After all, the resident inmates are troubled individuals with often-violent histories who may be out of reach of even the most aggressive of rehabilitation efforts, and the separation from the outside world can in turn bring forth the very worst in them. Similar to all other prisons throughout the country, violence and death have been prevalent within the walls of the Lackawanna County Jail since its conception, and some inmates have died by execution, suicide, assault by other inmates and even natural causes. As mentioned previously, the tormented or agitated emotional states of the prisoners and their violent deaths could serve as a catalyst for future hauntings. Some colorful legends exist regarding the building, including that the spirit of one of the old wardens still makes his rounds in the corridors of the prison at night. Although these claims remain to be proven, the following true story involving a former guard at the prison suggests that there may indeed be some truth behind them.

Late one night, while working alone at a guard station in the women's ward, a female officer was suddenly snapped to attention by the sound of intense screaming coming from one of the nearby cells. The officer unlocked the door to the cellblock and hurried down the corridor to where the screaming was coming from. She was worried that a few of the inmates were involved in a fight and were hurting one another, so she prepared herself for anything. When the officer arrived at the cell in question, she instead found a very startled female inmate huddled in the corner of her cell. After a few moments of coaxing from the officer, the hysterical woman calmed down enough to relate what had gotten her so worked up. She said that she was sleeping and suddenly woke up to see the face of strange man pressed up against the glass of the small porthole in her cell door. The man did not say anything and was just staring at her intensely with a savage look in his eyes. The

Front view of the new Lackawanna County Jail with original staff members. Note that the adjacent road was under construction. *Courtesy of the Lackawanna Historical Society.*

inmate was certain that he meant her harm and was afraid that he would somehow get into the cell with her, so she began screaming for help. The guard was confused by this since she was sitting in front of the only door to the cellblock where the prisoner was located and had let no one in or out for the entire night. In addition, the guard had seen no one in the corridor where the cell was located when heading to the cell and upon further investigation afterward. She thought at first that the inmate was lying, but the reaction and present condition of the woman seemed genuine enough. When the officer revealed that no one could have possibly been in the hallway and suggested

A photograph of the Lackawanna County Jail, circa the late 1880s, taken from near the current-day intersection of North Washington Avenue and New York Street. Note the horse-drawn carriage and the constable standing on the corner. *Courtesy of the Lackawanna Historical Society.*

that the inmate had probably just had a vivid nightmare, the rattled woman shook her head and said that the intruder was the ghost of a man who had been seen recently by other female inmates in the ward. Maybe the woman's experience was only a bad dream, but perhaps she had seen the spirit of the old warden or a male inmate who had died in the prison.

4

THE HOTEL JERMYN

LEAVE THE GHOST LIGHT ON FOR ELEANOR

In the nearly 120 years since its construction, the massive seven-story building located at 326 Spruce Street has been one of the true defining landmarks of the city of Scranton. Although its role has changed over time, the Hotel Jermyn has long stood by as a steadfast witness to the majority of the city's early industrial booms, growth, development, elated times and tragic events. This Romanesque-style structure was designed by architect John A. Duckworth and built on the former location of the preceding Forest House hotel by an English immigrant and mine owner named John Jermyn, who first came to the United States in 1847 and later opened the first privately owned mine in the Scranton area. Eventually, his successful individual mining operations allowed him the opportunity of owning a large portion of real estate in the area and constructing two of the city's most premier buildings: the Coal Exchange Building (also designed by Duckworth) and the Hotel Jermyn.

The Forest House, named for the section of dense woodland that was cut down at the location to construct the building itself, was built around 1855 for use as a boardinghouse. Several years afterward, the three-story building was sold and later expanded to have a fourth floor after becoming a highly popular regular service hotel. However, due to the rapid growth of the city at this time, the Forest House was eventually demolished to

The Hotel Jermyn decorated for Independence Day, circa the early 1900s. *Courtesy of the Lackawanna Historical Society.*

make way for the new, improved and much larger Hotel Jermyn. The new hotel was designed to be completely fireproof and was composed entirely of brick and stone on a frame of structural steel. Wood was utilized in the construction of only door and window trimmings, and the original doors and furnishings were made of metal. Building construction of this nature was becoming popular in the city due to the local abundance of required raw materials, as well as the strong presence of the industries that processed them. The construction of the Hotel Jermyn started in 1894 and took approximately two years to complete. On April 20, 1895, the unfinished building experienced its own unfortunate tragedy when a carpenter named Charlie Weiss fell eighty feet to his death while working on the looming structure.

By the early 1900s, successful industry had forever altered the Scranton area from a mere wilderness inhabited by local natives into a truly modern and cosmopolitan city with a large number of successful businesses, elegant shops, prominent buildings and bustling streets. The Hotel Jermyn certainly added to this general ambiance in the city when it officially opened to the public on April 8, 1896, and its lavish and elegant interior was first observed by at least ten thousand eager visitors. The hotel contained 250 guest rooms with hot and cold running water, 100 rooms with private baths, steam heat and electric light and gas throughout the building. John Jermyn hired Joseph Godfrey, the manager of the former Forest House, to run the daily operations of the new hotel, which soon became an extremely popular source of local high-class lodging for businessmen and performers who traveled across the county with agendas of business and pleasure. At this time, entertainment played an important part in the culture of the city, and Scranton contained numerous theaters where one could whet his or her appetite with anything from plays and minstrel shows to full opera performances. The acts were required to have cutting-edge material since the dubious Scranton audiences were widely known to be difficult to appease due to their desire for quality entertainment in return for their hard-earned money. Throughout the years of operation as a hotel, the building hosted a vast number of famous actors, actresses, bandleaders and historical figures within its walls, and some of the entertainers even performed at the local theaters while in Scranton. Even the thirty-fourth president of the United States, Dwight D. Eisenhower, once stayed at the hotel while visiting the city. In order to entertain the city locals and high-profile guests, the hotel once housed a much-loved nightclub called the Omar Room, which featured its own twenty-six-piece orchestra ensemble.

John Jermyn died on May 29, 1902, at the age of seventy-two. Eventually, the managers of the Jermyn estate sold the hotel to George Maxey and Frank P. Benjamin in 1923. In 1997, the building's function was changed to serve as permanent residential apartments for the elderly and disabled. To date, the structure is still largely used for this purpose, with a few exceptions. The now-defunct Electric City Theatre

The Hotel Jermyn in its heyday, circa the mid-1900s. *Courtesy of the Lackawanna Historical Society.*

Company converted one of the original hotel ballrooms into a small theater, which hosted local plays and dramatic events throughout the year. It is here that the underlying paranormal history of the building was uncovered—or revived.

Ghosts and the theater have been eternally linked throughout the ages from the days of the early Shakespearean performances (and possibly before) right up into modern times. It is common theatrical superstition that every theater has at least one resident ghost, and much of the strange and unexplained phenomena that are experienced in the theaters of today are attributed in some way to those spirits. In some instances, it is deemed good luck for an actor or performer to catch a glimpse of a theater spirit, such as the paradigm of the Drury Lane Theatre ghosts in London, England. Some of the ghosts in this particular theater are helpful and attempt to assist or calm nervous actors prior to their performances. Drury Lane's most famous spirit, called the "man in grey," is said to bestow extraordinary success on any performer fortunate enough to see him. In other cases, the theater phantoms are viewed as malevolent entities that could potentially wreak havoc about the set and/or sabotage the current production. It is believed by superstitious theater operators that the act of setting up a ghost light during closed hours, when the theater is entirely dark, is a way to appease these harmful spirits. This ghost light is usually just a single bare-bulb lamp that is left on in the middle of the stage all night. Since the resident ghosts are thought to be the ethereal forms of actors or performers who had an association with the theater in life, the ghost light provides a way to satisfy their eternal desire to keep performing on stage within the limelight. Conversely, in the days of old, candle ghost lights were burned on the stage in an effort to keep ghosts away from the performances and actors.

There are also many practical explanations for the use of ghost lights within a theater, the first being for the safety of anyone walking on the darkened stage after hours who would not wish to suffer an injury by falling off the stage or tripping over props or pieces of the set. Keeping a light on at night would also allow one to find his or her way around the building effectively and could also provide the theater with some protection against liability if an event such as those previously described were to occur. In addition, prior to the modern conveniences of today, theaters were once illuminated by the use of coal gas lamps, and keeping a pilot flame burning at all times would prevent the buildup of pressure within the gas lines, which could potentially result in an explosion of the coal gas generator. In the 1800s, a large number of famous theaters burned to the ground due to this scenario before harnessed electricity and the light bulb were introduced as a means of interior building illumination.

The staff of the Electric City Theatre Company, once located within the Hotel Jermyn, also adheres to the age-old tradition and superstitions regarding the operation of a ghost light within the theater, and for good reason. After moving into the building, some strange and supposed supernatural occurrences had been witnessed by some of the theater staff, as well as some of the event performers. Psychics, mediums and other sensitive individuals who entered the theater honed in on the presence of several resident spirits in the building, including the carpenter mentioned earlier who died during the construction of the building and a local priest/actor with a love for theater who died of a heart attack while performing onstage. However, the most infamous and well-known ghost amongst the staff is undoubtedly a female spirit called Eleanor.

Surprisingly, older workers and residents in the other sections of the building utilized as apartments for the elderly and disabled had known this particular spirit long before the Electric City Theater Company established a presence in the Hotel Jermyn. Although no one dwelling or working within the structure today knows exactly how the spirit got her name or who she really was in life, many still acknowledge Eleanor's presence and mention her name when something out of the ordinary happens in the building. Eleanor is thought to be the spirit of an actress or performer from the 1920s or '30s who tragically died while staying at the hotel. The unfortunate woman is believed to have had a fatal fall out one of the windows on the sixth or seventh floor of the building. A number of legend followers believe that Eleanor's death was a mere accident or perhaps a suicide. However, others surmise that her death could have been the result of something much more dark and sinister—like murder.

Those who believe in the latter theory claim that Eleanor was a strikingly beautiful actress or dancer who traveled to Scranton regularly to perform in the local theaters. She eventually attracted the attention of a Scranton man of prominence and power who was possibly a successful businessman or a politician. Even though he was married, the two began a lustful and covert affair that could have lasted as long as several years. Eventually, Eleanor discovered that she had become pregnant with the man's child and confronted him about the situation one night in her guest room at the Hotel Jermyn. The man was shocked by the news and desperately searched his panic-stricken mind for a way to resolve the matter without his affair becoming public knowledge and ruining his reputation in the community. Eleanor's unyielding decision to keep the child did not help matters in the eyes of her lover, and the initial discussion evolved into a heated argument between the two. The man became so enraged at Eleanor that he committed the ultimate of sins in a brash attempt to erase his mistake from the world. He pushed her out the window of her sixth- or seventh-floor guest room, and she fell to her death on the sidewalk below. After the murder, this man of power could have covered up any potential leads or ties to him with bribe money.

The above story is indeed one possibility, and even though no tangible evidence has been discovered to date regarding the death of a woman named Eleanor in the building, her legend has still managed to survive to this day. Has it all been due to the imaginations of people and their willingness to believe in a fantastic story, or is there more substance here? The following paranormal experiences of the staff within the theater portion of the building may suggest that the legend is more than just a coincidence or fabricated tale. The theater staff had explained that on more than one occasion while discussing the legend or possible murder of Eleanor, nearby lights in the theater have immediately flickered or turned off completely. People who have experienced this phenomenon claim that Eleanor is attempting to communicate or possibly suggest clues to explain what happened to her.

Eleanor is well known throughout the building as a harmless prankster spirit that is often responsible for misplacing small items belonging to the theater staff and performers. A few years ago, a local actress and member of the theater staff was having some trouble locating a particularly important stage prop that was needed for her part in a performance that was taking place later that day. The item was a hairbrush, and she had been warned by her superiors to keep it in a safe place until the show started. Up until this point, she had been most careful in keeping track of the location of the brush, but suddenly she discovered that it was not where she had last left it. The actress searched everywhere in her dressing room and could not find it. She asked everyone she came upon if they had seen the prop and turned the theater upside down searching for it, but no one claimed to know where it was, and it never turned up. After many minutes of frantic searching, the actress returned to her dressing room, defeated and dejected by the thought of losing the prop. She had no idea what she was going to tell her superiors about the matter, let alone what she could use in place of the brush during the performance. Finally, she remembered the seemingly far-fetched story of the building's resident and trickster ghost Eleanor, which she had learned about from the other staff members and performers at the theater. The actress did not believe in ghosts and thought that the tale was just made up to generate a creepy ambiance for the theater. However, in a last-ditch effort to recover the brush, the actress asked out loud in her dressing room that Eleanor please return the brush because she desperately needed it for the performance. Several minutes later, the actress turned around and was utterly astounded to see the very brush she had been looking for resting on the lid of the trash can in her room. She had specifically checked this location earlier when she lifted the lid to look through the discarded items inside the can in case the brush had been accidentally thrown out. From that day on, the actress exclaimed that the experience had definitely caused her to reevaluate the possibility of the existence of ghosts and the presence of Eleanor in the building.

Despite the numerous instances of misplaced belongings, flickering lights and other antics attributed to Eleanor in the building, few people claim to have actually seen this spirit. Unfortunately for her, a seven-year-old girl who had a history of being sensitive to spirits and was present to perform in a play at the Hotel Jermyn several years ago did spot Eleanor. Immediately before events in the theater, it is common for the performers to prepare for their routine in the adjacent ballroom. On this particular night, the youth was doing some last-minute preparations in the ballroom with the assistance of her mother. The girl was concentrating on the routine and focusing on her mother when something appeared in her peripheral vision, stealing the girl's attention. She suddenly turned to face the bar area and gasped, pointing at the large mirrors hanging from the walls. "Mommy, who is that lady?" the girl exclaimed in a frightened voice. The mother turned to face the mirror but saw only her own reflection and that of her daughter. The girl went on to describe seeing

The former main ballroom, called the Keystone Room, inside the Hotel Jermyn, circa the 1960s. *Courtesy of the Lackawanna Historical Society.*

the image of a woman whose clothing was more indicative of the 1930s era than modern times.

In addition, a veteran actress from out of town who was cast for a lead position in a series of performances at the theater claimed to experience strong feelings of dread, fear and trepidation while onstage in the Hotel Jermyn. She also often felt that she was being watched by a spirit that she believed felt ill will toward her while in the theater. The actress admitted to seeing the image of a woman standing alone in the rear of the theater on several occasions; she linked this to a feeling of uneasiness. Eventually, the woman became so uncomfortable in the Hotel Jermyn that she broke a lucrative contract with the production company that had hired her just so she would not have to perform there any longer. Perhaps this was Eleanor's way of preventing another actress from stealing her prominent role at the Hotel Jermyn.

5

THE BANSHEE PUB

BEWARE OF THE BASEMENT

The unassuming three-story brick building at 320 Penn Avenue is among the most haunted in the Electric City. Perhaps not by coincidence, the building is the present home of the Banshee Pub, an old-fashioned Irish-themed pub named after a female spirit in Irish mythology usually seen as an omen of death. The name is oddly suitable since many people frequenting this location have experienced strange occurrences there, including the sighting of ghosts. No one really knows the specific reasons multiple spirits linger in the building, but there is a degree of speculation as to their origin. However, to tell their story, we must go back to a tumultuous period of history when the city of Scranton, Pennsylvania, and the rest of the world were enduring one of the worst pandemics in human history.

In the summer of 1918, an unusually severe and deadly illness began spreading like wildfire across the globe from the Arctic to remote Pacific islands. It killed people more quickly than any other known disease in history. To this day, medical science does not know exactly how the disease originated or where it went after running its course. However, what is known is that it claimed over twice as many lives worldwide in six months than did World War I in four years. The illness was a dangerous outbreak of the H1N1 influenza virus, which

The Banshee Pub, located at 320 Penn Avenue, is one of the most haunted locations in the city of Scranton. *Photo by Olivia Bernardi.*

lasted from June 1918 to December 1920 and killed between 50 and 100 million people worldwide. Unfortunately, the spread of the virus was vastly accelerated due to the close quarters and massive troop movements involved with World War I, as well as increased travel due to modern transportation. The illness was incorrectly dubbed the "Spanish flu" due to the fact that Spain was a neutral country at the time of the war and provided no censorship of news regarding the disease or the severity of its impact there. Other countries aligned with the Central Powers and the Allied Powers did not disclose news of the illness through the media because they did not want to release any information about death tolls to their enemies or lower their own troops' morale.

The strange part was that unlike most influenza outbreaks, the majority of victims were healthy young adults with strong immune systems instead of the usual targets consisting of children and the elderly. The reason for this was because the virus caused a severe overreaction of the immune system, which ravaged the body of young adults but was not nearly as effective on the weaker immune systems of the older and the very young. The illness started with a cough and then quickly escalated with pain behind the eyes and ears and an uncomfortable increase in body temperature, heart rate and respiration. Soon, pneumonia followed as the lungs became inflamed and then filled with liquid, finally suffocating the victims.

In September 1918, the black tendrils of the virus began reaching into the more populated cities of Pennsylvania, including Philadelphia and Pittsburgh, and had quickly climbed to epidemic proportions by October 4, 1918. Attempts were made to limit exposure to the contagion by banning public gatherings and closing schools, churches, places of amusement and theaters, but this did not prove an effective prevention. Pharmacy shelves were stripped bare by frantic shoppers looking for a means to treat their illness. The Philadelphia College of Pharmacy and Temple University suspended classes to allow pharmacy students to assist with the filling of prescriptions, which mostly included whiskey (the only treatment prescribed for influenza), now only available in drugstores since the closing of taverns in the city. As a result, pharmacists raised the price of whiskey to fifty-two dollars a gallon, and the ferries became overcrowded with a mass exodus of people desperately trying to reach Camden, New Jersey, where the taverns remained open. Snake oil salesmen emerged to hawk their phony remedies in newspaper ads and on the streets. There was a severe influx of patients to the hospitals, which were vastly understaffed due to the large numbers of doctors and nurses called into military duty for World War I. The local hospitals sent out for volunteers to relieve nurses who had collapsed from overwork.

The living conditions became horrific with the climbing death toll as city administrators, policemen, firemen and garbage collectors became ill and could not perform their duties. In October, the city of Pittsburgh experienced a shortage of coffins to bury the dead, and the Philadelphia morgue held over ten times the amount of bodies it was designed to handle. Over seven hundred people died of the disease on October 16 alone in Philadelphia. Volunteers driving horse-drawn wagons were dispatched throughout the city to collect unburied bodies from individual homes. These bodies were tagged for identification and buried at Potter's Field, where the Bureau of Highways dug trenches for the graves. Survivors at the time were told that the bodies of their loved ones could be reinterred when the threat of the epidemic ended so they would relinquish the bodies without argument. Despite the extensive efforts to collect the bodies, the dead were not being buried fast enough, the Office of the Coroner could not keep up with the demand for death certificates and cold-storage plants were being utilized as temporary morgues. To make more money, some cemeteries and undertakers raised the price of burial services to obscene amounts. As an emergency course of action, convicts were ordered to bury the bodies of the dead, which were stacked and rotting in the hallways of the Philadelphia morgue, and five other supplementary morgues were opened up to receive even more bodies.

By October 25, official estimates declared that over 350,000 cases of the illness existed in Pennsylvania, and it was not long until the disease struck the anthracite region of the state, which included the city of Scranton. At the peak of the 1918 influenza pandemic, the Electric City experienced similar conditions to those in Philadelphia since it was one of the larger cities in Pennsylvania, with a population of around 140,000. Newspaper articles obtained from the *Scranton Times* during that period explain that funeral parlors could not keep up with the demand for services and that local businesses with space were being asked to temporarily house the bodies of victims until they could receive proper burials. A dry goods store named Eisner and Sons, located at 320 Penn Avenue, was one of the local businesses in the city at the time that could have been used for this purpose. In fact, although official documentation cannot be found to date, during a 2008 interview the previous owners of the Banshee Pub insisted that the basement of the building was used as a temporary morgue in 1918.

The present exterior of the three-story brick building at 320 Penn Avenue appears close to what it looked like back in 1918, with the exception of the Irish-themed façade of the popular tavern on the first level. Upon gazing at the upper stories of the building, one can get true a sense of what it felt like walking through the city nearly one hundred years ago. At that time, Penn Avenue was a much more bustling street than it is nowadays, and the Scranton Private Hospital was located almost directly behind the building on the corner of Mulberry Street and Wyoming Avenue. The hospital was started in 1895 by Dr. Charles E. Thompson, and although the original building does not exist anymore, in 1918 the Scranton Private Hospital was one of the oldest and most successful private hospitals in the region at that time, noted for its breakthroughs in abdominal surgery, its exceptional nursing school and its specializations in care for patients suffering with ailments from almost any affliction or accident conceivable.

The *Scranton Times* newspaper documented that the Scranton Private Hospital received and treated patients suffering from influenza in the fall of 1918. If bodies of the deceased victims were indeed temporarily stored in the basement of the Eisner and Sons building prior to interment, transportation of the bodies would have been convenient since only a narrow alley separated the buildings. In addition, the 1918 city directory revealed that a funeral parlor existed at 320 Franklin Avenue, only one block away from the Eisner and Sons building. This helps to certify the possibility of a temporary morgue at 320 Penn Avenue since the building fit the profile for use and was so close to both a hospital and a funeral parlor.

To this day, it is believed that the restless spirits of some Scranton residents who perished during the 1918 influenza pandemic still haunt the old Eisner and Sons building at 320 Penn Avenue. This belief has yet to be proven, but it is a major part of the lore of the building since its opening in the year 2000. On the inside, the building contains many remnants of a bygone era, including a fifty-foot-long wooden bar located on the first floor, as well as many tables and bookshelves constructed of wood salvaged from the original building interior. There is even an old-fashioned functioning elevator used by the current employees to travel from floor to floor, complete with a sparking power source that appears right out of a Frankenstein movie.

A creaky wooden staircase ascends from the picturesque main bar room with its high engraved tin ceilings to an equally antiquated-

The first-floor bar area of the Banshee Pub. The beautifully crafted fifty-foot-long wooden bar was constructed from the original shelves of the Eisner and Sons dry goods store. *Courtesy of the Banshee Pub.*

looking second floor that is home to a smaller bar area and a banquet room. A storage area resides on the darkened third floor that houses a vast array of decorations and antiques used for the pub. The cold stone floor and block walls of the basement engulf you in an eerie and oppressive silence upon entry and make it seem as though the merriment being had just one floor above is miles away. The larger main area of the space houses a pair of walk-in coolers, as well as a stockpile of beer and liquor. A smaller offshoot area of the basement known as "the vault" for its pair of antique metal double entry doors is located underneath the sidewalk in front of the building and is the most probable location where bodies could have been stored back in 1918. Employees of the pub say the basement is by far the most unnerving location in the building, where many of them do not wish to visit alone, or at all; it is the epicenter for the darkest and most violent brushes with the supernatural experienced at the pub.

Since the time of the pub's opening, many employees have experienced feelings of dread and being watched by unseen forces in the basement. It is a place where seemingly sentient shadows appear and disappear without warning or explanation. These shadows can be witnessed at times silently slithering across the walls in the peripheral vision of the observer or even in plain sight. According to modern ghost lore, dark silhouettes of deceased human spirits, called "shadow people," have been seen and photographed in haunted locations for years.

One particular worker told me of a violent encounter she had with one of these unseen forces in the basement on a summer evening. The employee was sent down to the basement to bring back a couple of six packs for the bar. Due to the warm weather, she was wearing a sleeveless shirt but was suddenly chilled to the bone when the air around her abruptly dropped in temperature. Within several moments, she began to feel a sharp and intense pain in her shoulder and was terrified enough to run back upstairs to the main bar area. After telling other employees of her experience in the basement, they noticed that the skin on one of her shoulders was turning red. The peculiar thing was that the reddish mark on her shoulder oddly resembled a human bite mark.

Other experiences in the pub related by employees and patrons alike include sightings of full-bodied apparitions on the first and second floors of the building. Some surprised people have witnessed the tall figure of a man wearing a dated-looking black overcoat and top hat standing at the bottom of the staircase on the first floor. He is said to be in his thirties or forties and just stares out into the main bar area for several moments with a lost look on his face before vanishing. Perhaps he is looking for help or is just simply confused by seeing the modern technology present in the bar and the peculiar clothing of the patrons. In any case, he does not usually stay long enough for anyone to find out what he wants. The correct term is "usually" because a story does exist about the pub involving this shadowy character that does not fit the common description. Several years ago, a mother with her young son of about eight or ten years stopped in the pub to have lunch. While ordering her selection, she became engrossed in a conversation with the waitress, who was an old friend or acquaintance. After several moments, she noticed that her son had left his seat. The woman stood up and began searching frantically for her son. She finally caught a glimpse of the top of his head disappear down the staircase leading into the basement. Both the mother and the waitress quickly followed the boy into the basement and found him standing alone near a wall. Visibly upset and confused about why her son had left without telling her, the mother questioned the boy and demanded the reason he had decided to head into the basement of the establishment. The boy, seeming a bit detached from reality at the moment, stated only that a man in black carrying a rope had asked the boy to follow him. The mother and the waitress scoured the basement for the mentioned man in black, but no one was found.

The other notable tale regarding a specific ghost at the Banshee involves a young girl around the age of four or five. She wears a stark white dress and is often seen in the second-floor banquet room and on the staircase to the third floor. Late at night, when the bar is empty or only a few patrons remain, her gleeful laughter can sometimes be heard echoing throughout the building. Some employees think they have heard her footsteps bounding up and down the staircases on occasion when no living person is present. No one really knows who she is, but all who have witnessed her presence agree she is friendly. The young girl's spirit seems to be at play in the building as she may have been in life.

In a 2008 interview, one employee of the pub described her first chilling encounter with the ghost of the young girl; it occurred several months after she was hired at the Banshee. Up until that time, she said that she did not believe the tales spun about the ghost by her co-workers and that she thought the stories were told just to frighten new employees. However, she adopted another view entirely upon witnessing the apparition of the young girl in the second-floor banquet room.

A private party had just ended in the room minutes before, and the guests had either all left or descended to the first-floor bar area.

The employee was in the process of cleaning up after the guests and was in the adjacent barroom when she heard the distinct laughter of a little girl. Thinking that someone from the party had left their child behind, she ran into the room to get the child and hopefully catch the parents before they exited the building. She was literally stunned speechless upon entering the banquet room when she saw the semitransparent image of a young girl in a white dress standing on the staircase to the third floor. The ghost looked at her for a few seconds and then proceeded up the stairs; she vanished from sight before reaching the top. Many others have seen this apparition, and some "sensitive" people frequenting the pub have admitted to feeling her presence, but no one seems to know exactly who this child is or why she lingers in the building.

After hearing the ghost stories about the bar told so passionately by its employees, it certainly does seem plausible that there might indeed be other "spirits" residing in the Banshee Pub in addition to the liquid

R. SCHOENFEELD,

UNDERTAKER,

AND DEALER IN

ALL KINDS OF FURNITURE,
320 PENN AVE., SCRANTON, PA.

An advertisement for 320 Penn Avenue taken from the 1879 Scranton City Directory. *Courtesy of the Lackawanna Historical Society.*

ones sold and imbibed at the fine establishment. The tales of ghostly sightings and encounters in the pub have existed for some time, and actual evidence to support their presence has since come to light. We may never know the real reason why these spirits remain at 320 Penn Avenue or who they were in life. They could have been victims of the 1918 influenza outbreak whose bodies were stored in the building and whose spirits never found the means to pass on from this world. Another interesting fact regarding the property was discovered in the 1879–1880 edition of the Scranton City Directory, which lists 320 Penn Avenue as the location of the R. Schoenfeeld undertaker business. This business also sold and manufactured wooden furniture and coffins. Perhaps this use of the building has something to do with the paranormal activity within. At any rate, the presence of ghosts in the building definitely adds to the ambiance of the pub and makes it an exciting destination for people in search of a good drink and a potential encounter with the spirit realm.

6

ANDY GAVIN'S EATERY AND PUB

A GHOST NAMED GEORGE

Approximately one mile from the heart of downtown Scranton is a building that houses one of the city's most famous and notorious spirits. The building's address is 1392 North Washington Avenue, and it rests directly across from the fortress-like Lackawanna County Prison on the corner of North Washington and the adjacent New York Street. The property's history can be traced back to at least 1887, before the land was developed. The beautiful three-story house with a wraparound porch and a cylindrical tower projecting from the second floor that currently resides on the property was constructed sometime between 1887 and 1890. Throughout the years, the building has undoubtedly seen several different uses—often multiple uses at one time—and countless people have passed though its doors for business, pleasure and residency.

The building was originally constructed as a private family dwelling and a physician's office for Dr. George E. Hill and his wife, Celia, most likely around the year 1890. The Hills sold the property in 1895 to James Kelley, who later converted the house into a hotel in 1905 and added JJ Kelley's Saloon in 1910. The property then changed hands again in 1922, going to the Calpin family, who used the building as a boardinghouse and tavern until 1971, when it was purchased by its current namesake: the Gavins. Since then, the property changed owners two more times, but the

Andy Gavin's Eatery and Pub, located at 1392 North Washington Avenue, is known for its mischievous resident spirit named George. *Photo by Olivia Bernardi.*

building's use as a tavern with upstairs rental apartments has remained consistent. Currently, the building consists of the popular Andy Gavin's Eatery and Pub on the first floor, an apartment dwelling on the second floor and storage space on the third floor.

The tales of encounters with spirits in this old house have been reported since at least the early 1980s, when the previous owner himself had a chilling brush with the supernatural while renovating the rooms on the second and third floors. The strangest and most memorable experience he had occurred shortly after purchasing the property, when he was in the process of painting the rooms on the upper two floors that were to become rental apartments. It was a very hot day, in the upper eighties to low nineties, with a high level of humidity—typical weather in the dead of summer in northeastern Pennsylvania. In an attempt to stave off the stifling heat, he had the windows open to let the trapped warm air out (since there was no air conditioning) and to provide adequate ventilation while painting. The heated working conditions were nearly unbearable on the upper floors of the house, and the open windows did practically nothing to improve the situation as he continued the tedious and daunting task alone.

Sweat beaded on his forehead and ran in a constant stream down his face. While painting on the third floor, he silently wished for some relief from the intense heat and was suddenly surprised when an ice-cold gust of air appeared from nowhere and wafted over him. He abruptly stopped working and glanced around for an explanation as to the source of the bone-chilling cold, which he explained felt like walking into a freezer. After several minutes of searching, he came up empty and thought that one of his friends had silently entered the house and was playing a practical joke on him. He called out to see if anyone was there with him and waited several moments, but there was no answer. Thinking that the unexplained drop in temperature was strange but finding no logical source, he brushed it off as his imagination and reluctantly returned to the third floor to continue his work.

Upon reaching the area where he had left off, the owner discovered that the chill had surprisingly passed as quickly as it had come upon him. However, within several minutes of continuing his work, the chill was upon him again, only this time there was more than just cold air present to rattle his senses. He distinctly heard a man's voice sound off very close to his right ear a few moments after feeling the cold air surround him for the second time. The owner exclaimed that the sudden alarming voice was loud but gruff and garbled. He did not discern what was said but was so frightened that he bolted out of the house as fast as his legs would carry him. The experience was so unsettling that he never ascended to the second or third floors of the building by himself from that day on and finally sold the property, nearly a decade later in 1988, to the current owner.

It was during this following, and now current, ownership of the property when the word "George" first surfaced as a possible name for the resident entity of the building. One night, the owner's son and some friends were having a party in the house and decided to entertain themselves in a different way by using a Ouija, or spirit, board. They were familiar with the legend of the ghost in the house and wanted to see if they could communicate with the entity by utilizing the device. The use of spirit boards is considered archaic and controversial at best in the field of modern paranormal investigation. Some people swear they are harmless toys for mild amusement, rightfully sold in the game section of department stores. Others consider spirit boards to be a very dangerous tool that should only be used when exercising extreme caution or, better yet, not used at all. The common belief behind all the danger is that the entities that are usually willing to communicate through the board are most likely to be tormented human spirits trapped at the location of their tragic demise, such as victims of suicides and murders; they are unhappy and restless and would/could not provide a very positive experience for the users of the board. In addition, other inhuman and evil spirits just hanging around in the darkness looking for opportunities to corrupt and hurt living people—such as demons— are also likely to be contacted in this manner. These evil spirits would initially try to trick the users into believing they were harmless, only to reveal their true intentions later, when it is too late.

Many cases of negative experiences with using spirit boards have been documented throughout recent history. There have been reported consequences for the users, including everything from property damage up to full spirit possessions of the living. Sometimes the contacted entities are not so willing to stop communication with the ending of the spirit board session, so they latch on to a user and hang around long enough to mess up their lives in some way, such as causing them emotional pain and depression or even taking over an aspect of their personality. Indeed, the potential results of using spirit boards should be warning enough not to use them; however, some people are perhaps too foolish or curious to steer clear of the device.

During this party in the house, the users of the Ouija board believe that they first contacted and communicated with the building's resident ghost. When the enthralled youths asked the spirit its name, the planchette (a heart-shaped pointer) slowly moved to the individual letters on the board to spell out the name "George." After this particular night, the owner's son was so amazed at the thought of openly communicating with the spirit world that he had numerous other sessions with the board, which divulged additional information about the spirit haunting the house. The painstaking use of the board provided some possible answers as to what had happened to George during his life and why he had remained in the building. It was discovered that he was a coal miner who lived in the home during the late 1800s. He supposedly committed suicide by hanging himself on one of the upper floors of the building. Later on, the owner's son and the others who had been frequently using the Ouija board soon learned that the spirit they were communicating with was the tormented soul of a man who had died in the house and was forever trapped within. It soon became evident to the youths that George was angry at his current predicament and frustrated by the slow and inefficient method of communication provided by the spirit board. The sessions with him became increasingly more frightening than fun as George found new ways of emphasizing his ideas—such as flickering the lights—so the owner's son decided to break off the communication all together. He sought out the aid of a local priest, who blessed the board and told him to burn it, which he willingly did. Since that time, the owner, with the help of several priests, has attempted to cleanse the building of spirits, but to no avail. To this day, evidence of the presence of George still remains in the building. However, he is considered by the current owner and staff to be a mischievous but harmless ghost.

In addition to all the sudden unexplained drops in temperature, disembodied voices and spirit board activity, the current staff at Andy Gavin's Eatery and Pub has also experienced a good share of poltergeist activity in the building since the bar reopened under new ownership in 1988. *Poltergeist* is a word of German origin that essentially translates to "noisy spirit." This sort of paranormal activity can consist of the movement of inanimate objects, disembodied sounds and even violent physical attacks on the living people who witness the phenomena. The unfortunate onlookers never see the actual spirit, but its emotional essence is physically manifested through affecting the surrounding environment. The poltergeist often hurls clusters of small, normally stationary objects through the air; produces disembodied groans, moans and banging noises; and causes electrical malfunctions in household appliances and lights. Throughout the ages, some scientists have theorized many potential causes for poltergeist activity outside the spiritual realm, including geomagnetism, seismic activity and even telekinesis, but the true source of the phenomena has yet to be explained. However, since it often occurs in reputably haunted locations, it is a common belief of paranormal researchers that poltergeist activity can be the result of a malevolent spirit attempting to manifest, communicate or just wreak havoc. Sometimes this activity can be far subtler, even sneaky, and cause stranger things to happen like the following events that have occurred on more than several occasions at Andy Gavin's Eatery and Pub.

The employees of the pub stated that after the bar is closed every night, it is common practice to clean the kitchen, the bar, the floors and all of the tables and then stack the chairs upside down on the tables. Often, the next step is to turn off most of the electronics and lights on the bar level and then proceed to the basement, where the office is located, for some end-of-the-day financial work. While in the office, the remaining employees claim not to hear anything occurring upstairs, and everybody else on the bar level has left, with all the doors to the outside locked from the inside. On one occasion, upon ascending the stairs to the bar level from the basement after completing their work in the office, these remaining workers were shocked to find that some of the previously stacked chairs were now sitting upright in the middle of the floor, and some tables had been moved several feet from their usual resting places. There was no apparent cause for the movement, which should have made a noise loud enough to hear from the floor directly below. In addition, some of the lights that had been turned off by the employees just minutes before were switched on again. The employees claimed that this also often happens with the jukebox, and they are startled when it suddenly turns back on unexpectedly after being physically shut down. When this happens, they say that it's just George messing around with them.

Numerous patrons of the pub have also witnessed some strange and unexplainable things while visiting the establishment, such as silverware leaping off tables by itself, being touched by a chilling unseen force and actually seeing a full-bodied apparition of a male spirit in his thirties or forties (the latter being far less common). It seems that George also likes to play pranks on some of the male guests while they are in the men's restroom. Many have claimed to experience a feeling of uneasiness or of being watched by an unseen force when using the facilities in this small lavatory, which only includes a single urinal, toilet stall and sink. Others have said to witness the door of the stall actually shut and latch by itself while they are alone in the restroom washing their hands at the sink or using the urinal. The toilet in this restroom has also been known to flush by itself on occasion. However, it appears as though George does not limit his interaction with the living to only the first floor of the building. Tenants renting the second-floor apartment have reported feeling intense, unexplainable cold spots, which begin and end suddenly without warning, and have returned home to find their furniture moved to a new location apparently by itself.

Despite all the paranormal activity experienced in the building and the well-known legend of George, the spirit's true identity and reason(s) for haunting the place remain as somewhat of a mystery to this day. An obvious first possibility for the ghost's identity could be Dr. George E. Hill, since he bears a first name identical to the infamous ghost. In addition, he could also have a strong spiritual tie to the house since he was responsible for its construction and was one of the first people to live there. However, Dr. Hill's background does not fit into the legend behind the ghost since he was not a coal miner, did not die in the house and lived to the ripe old age of seventy-two. True evidence of an untimely death on the property has not yet come to light, but the building did have many residents throughout its history, and it is possible that one of the previous tenants in the early 1900s could have taken his life in one of the upstairs apartments. At that time, the modern obituary, as we have come to know it, did not yet exist, and the person's family, as well as the building's owner/operator, may have kept the cause of death out of the public light for obvious reasons. It is also possible that the spirit contacted by the use of the spirit board could have provided a false name or the name of someone else he knew who was connected with the property. It is common for trapped or tormented spirits to be confused, and they sometimes cannot remember specific details about their former lives or how they died. This "amnesia" could very well include basic information such as their own names. With this in mind, perhaps George is not this spirit's name after all.

Although the antics of George may definitely be considered odd and unnerving to some people, those who work in the pub or spend a good deal of time there truly feel that he means no harm and is just trying to let the living world know that he is still with us. Who knows, he might even enjoy the atmosphere of this fine establishment so much that he does not ever want to leave.

7

The Scranton Cultural Center at the Masonic Temple

MASONIC GHOSTS

Located at 420 Washington Avenue, the Scranton Cultural Center at the Masonic Temple has been one of the most iconic historical buildings in the city for over eighty years. Construction of this magnificent structure began in 1927 and was completed in 1930. The building is truly an exquisite masterpiece of architectural design and engineering. On the exterior, the looming stone structure appears as something straight out of ancient times or a fantasy movie, with its highly detailed stonework in Indiana limestone containing carvings of dragons and Masonic symbols. This grand building was erected on the site of the former home of Thomas Dickson, who at the time was the owner of the Dickson Manufacturing Company located on Penn Avenue and Vine Street. It is now the Pennsylvania Paper Supply Company. It should be noted that the block surrounding the Scranton Cultural Center contains many beautiful and historic buildings relative to the city's past that have been wonderfully preserved to this day.

On the corner of North Washington Avenue, immediately adjacent to the Cultural Center, is the older Albright Memorial Library, built in 1893. The library was designed by Buffalo architects Green and Wicks in the French Chateau style and is similar to the Cluny Museum in Paris. The building's exterior is also beautifully trimmed with detailed carvings in Indiana limestone, such as owls to signify the wisdom to gain from the numerous volumes of books inside and lions to protect the entrance. The library originally had outside gardens designed by the noted landscape architect Frederick Law Olmsted, who was famous for his design of Central and Prospect Parks in New York. These gardens were not established until 1995, when the original Olmsted plans were rediscovered and the gardens were implemented to their original intended glory. The architecture of the library and the Cultural Center complement one another and are harmonious to the extent that the windows and floor levels appear to line up on the exterior of the buildings. The property on which the library is built formerly contained the home of Joseph Albright, an early successful businessman in Scranton. Albright later relocated to Buffalo, New York. His family donated the land to construct the library.

The Scranton Cultural Center was designed by Raymond Hood, one of the most prominent architects of his time. Hood was renowned for his previous work in New York City, where he designed Rockefeller Center. The building was originally constructed as the Masonic Temple and Scottish Rite Cathedral, and the neo-Gothic and Romanesque style in which it was designed is a tribute to Masonry. Freemasonry is an extremely old fraternal society that even today has lodges or temples spread out all over the world and ideals that date well back to ancient times. It is a unique organization because it does not exist to make money and is not involved with any religious or political regime. In Europe, from the age of the great Charlemagne up to the days of the Reformation, the tradesmen who were trained in the craft of building to construct such items as barns and cottages were called masons. Furthermore, there were also those few special builders who could both design and construct monumental structures, including cathedrals, churches and town halls. These men were called freemasons (a word of similar meaning to architects today). When the need to design and construct a monumental public building arose, freemasons were summoned from all regions and even other countries to assist with the erection of the structure. Once a sufficient number of freemasons had arrived at the location, they built a meeting lodge of their own and

The former dwelling of Thomas Dickson, owner of the Dickson Manufacturing Company, whose family later donated the property for construction of the Masonic Temple and Scottish Rite Cathedral. *Courtesy of the Scranton Cultural Center at the Masonic Temple.*

The original dwellings demolished for the construction of the Masonic Temple and Scottish Rite Cathedral. *Courtesy of the Scranton Cultural Center at the Masonic Temple.*

cottages to house their families until construction of the monumental building was completed. Since these men often came separately from great distances, they could not have a permanent organization of their own like the local craftsmen, so they developed a fraternal society to stay connected and uphold their ideals, regulations and customs. The modern freemasonry practiced in lodges today across America is a direct descendant of this early fraternity and is so prevalent that most places, from large cities to small towns and villages, have at least one functioning Masonic lodge.

Prior to 1928, the Masonic order in the city utilized an old armory building for years as the headquarters for meetings and ceremonies, but they eventually desired a more suitable home or temple for the fraternity's needs. The local order finally got their wish when the design was completed, and bids for construction were taken in January 1927. Following the construction, the inauguration of the building, along with

The Masonic Temple and Scottish Rite Cathedral during construction, June 1928. *Courtesy of the Scranton Cultural Center at the Masonic Temple.*

The front entrance of the completed Masonic Temple and Scottish Rite Cathedral. *Courtesy of the Scranton Cultural Center at the Masonic Temple.*

the first meeting of the local Masonic Order, took place on January 2, 1930. Eventually, the Masonic Order decided to utilize the building for more public and community services, so a nonprofit organization was created to preserve the physical structure of the Masonic Temple and to provide an ongoing source for public programming and entertainment within the building. Over time, this successful campaign led to the renaming of the building to what it is known as today: the Scranton Cultural Center at the Masonic Temple.

The 180,000-square-foot rectangular building is composed of a structural steel frame surrounded by an exterior of Indiana limestone and has ten floors, of which only five are accessible by elevator. It contains two theaters, several meeting halls and a grand ballroom, in addition to numerous other storage and other purpose rooms. More interestingly, there is a fifteen-foot-diameter light room at the

The card room of the Scranton Cultural Center. *Courtesy of the Scranton Cultural Center at the Masonic Temple.*

very top of the building that can be reached only by the use of a ladder and a sub-basement that extends nearly sixty feet below the basement floor.

The picturesque Harry and Jeannette Weinberg Theater located on the ground floor of the Scranton Cultural Center can seat a maximum of 1,866 people for any one of the various events held there throughout the year, ranging from Broadway performances to stand-up comedy acts. Just sitting in this old-fashioned theater seems to provoke the mind into feeling transported back through time to an earlier period in American history. After experiencing this ambiance, one can't help but ponder the possibility that some guests present in the crowd might just be ghosts of a bygone era. The actual truth is that at least one of the seats in this theater is reserved for a guest who departed this life many years ago but still returns from time to time for some good entertainment. This spirit is known to the staff of the

Scranton Cultural Center as Sarah, and she most often occupies a seat in the small private balcony area to the left of the stage.

Over the years, many staff members and guests have glanced up from the orchestra level of the theater, or over from the rear balcony area, and were surprised to witness strange sights ranging from unexplained eerie lights and shadows to transparent images of a young girl sitting there looking at the stage. She is seen here most often during events when this area is not being used to seat guests. However, this spirit is sometimes witnessed by the cleaning crew or staff members after-hours or when the theater is empty. This small balcony, as well as the matching one located directly on the other side of the stage, is separated from the other seating areas in the theater and has its own staircase from the lower level. These balconies contain only a handful of seats and are usually utilized for private and reserved seating during certain events.

On one occasion several years ago, during a concert when this balcony was not being utilized to seat guests, one member of the Lackawanna Historical Society in attendance at the show said he observed a faint bluish white light glowing within the darkened balcony. The glow appeared suddenly sometime after the show began and lasted nearly until the end. Familiar with the legend of Sarah, he could not keep his fascinated gaze away from the unexplained light throughout the concert. The man kept studying the glow from his rear balcony seat, even though it caused him to miss the majority of a most-anticipated show for which he had purchased a ticket. After diligently trying to discern the source of the light for over an hour, he ultimately came to the decision that the origin of the glow was definitely not from any of the stage lights or from any another logical light source that was part of the show or the theater itself. In addition, he had seen no one in the small balcony for the entire show, so it could not have been a staff member, security guard or a guest using a flashlight or something similar during the event. Ultimately, his conclusion was firm: Sarah had also been a guest at the concert on that particular night.

The members of the Scranton Cultural Center staff who follow the legend of this spirit say that the true identity of Sarah is a bit of a mystery, and they are not sure if that is even her real name. However, Sarah has made her presence known enough in the theater to reveal that she appears to be a Caucasian girl of at least eight to ten years of age. She is believed to have been the daughter or relative of someone prominent in the Scranton area or even one of the original operators of the building in the 1930s and 1940s. During life, Sarah might have attended many classic events in the building back in Scranton's heyday, when the structure was young. She may have thus decided to revisit her beloved theater from time to time even after death. Whatever the reason, it is agreed that her presence within the historic Scranton Cultural Center certainly adds to the pronounced magical feeling.

Spirit mediums who have walked through the grand halls and rooms of the building say that it is not only home to some resident intelligent spirits but also teems with the intense spirit energy of people who have visited there long before. The energy is not only restricted to the theater but also permeates throughout the entire building, from the basement to the upper floors. This phenomenon is mostly due to the frequent use of this marvelous and popular building by large numbers of people over the last eighty years as a Masonic meeting hall, Scottish Rite Cathedral and a place for theatrical events. However, another surprising contributor is Indiana limestone, the very material from which the building is constructed. Limestone is widely believed in the field of the paranormal to be a substance that can store large amounts of residual spiritual energy. This residual energy is essentially composed of portions of significant events and emotions experienced by people once in the building. The energy has been captured in the stone walls and can essentially play back within the building at certain times and under the right conditions—not unlike small broken bits of film clips.

This is evident sometimes after-hours, when the theater is empty. Workers in the building often hear the sounds of young voices and children playing coming from the rear of the upper balcony area. At first, there is a veil of total silence in the darkened theater and then suddenly the quickened footsteps of small feet are heard, along with children laughing. The noises arise without warning and fade away almost as soon

The ballroom of the Scranton Cultural Center. *Courtesy of the Scranton Cultural Center at the Masonic Temple.*

as the witnesses realize what they are hearing, and upon investigation of the area, no children are ever found. Ironically, the staff members of the building revealed that back in the early days of the building, the children of the operators and high-ranking employees and their relatives used to play in the rear of the upper balcony level, underneath the projection booth, before and after performances in the theater. The children would often run back and forth between the isles of seats and play tag. Since no children have ever died in the theater or anywhere else in the building, it may seem odd that an echo of their essence still remains there to this day. The explanation may be as simple as the children played there often and had such a good time doing it that their joyful emotions were forever captured within the surrounding walls. Whatever the reason for their presence, the noises heard today bear a stark resemblance to what they are believed to be—the residual imprint of the children playing in the building many years ago.

On the second floor of the building, in a room that is now named the Casey Library, some unfortunate visitors and staff members have witnessed a startling visage that has been documented back to at least the 1960s. This apparition may be evidence of the residual spirit energy manifesting in the building. However, it could also be something else entirely, such as another resident intelligent spirit stalking the darkened rooms and corridors of the fortress-like structure. Every now and then, without warning, someone enters this room and is surprised to see a tall man clothed in a dark-colored or black cloak with the cowl pulled up over his head sitting in one of the chairs. This often happens when the person has just traversed through the seemingly empty room to the corridor beyond and returns several minutes later to find the ominous figure sitting down as if he had been stationed there for some time. The apparition is motionless, silent and appears with his head bowed as if he were intently reading, studying or perhaps even praying. In addition, the garb he wears closely resembles the ceremonial cloaks of the members of the Masonic order who have been present in the building since its construction and still hold gatherings there today. This spirit, perhaps lost in quiet reflection, never seems to take notice to the sudden intrusion despite how startled the onlooker may be, and he always vanishes just as suddenly and quietly as he appears. Witnesses never seem to feel directly threatened by the figure, but reactions have ranged from frightened running out of the room to passing through with a peculiar feeling that the cloaked man is strangely out of place. However, upon returning to the room for a second look, witnesses always find that the man has disappeared without a trace. Needless to say, the workers and guests at the Scranton Cultural Center who are familiar with this legend always enter the Casey Library with the anticipation of potentially seeing this ghostly figure.

The Scranton Cultural Center staff revealed that back in the early days of the building the present Casey Library was indeed utilized by the members of the Masonic order as a quiet study area. With this in mind, the description of the cloaked apparition that appears to be silently reading or reflecting does not seem out of place according to the history of the building. This mysterious figure could be the ghost of a former Mason who returns to the building from time to time to continue using the library, or it could be the residual imprint of a former Mason who spent so much time in the room during his life that some of his energy is forever trapped within the walls. Whatever the reason behind the presence of this apparition, discovering the truth of the matter may be as simple as just asking him the next time he appears. However, an individual brave enough has not been fortunate—or unfortunate—enough to cross paths with the dark-cloaked entity.

This building is truly magical inside and out, and many locals might say that there is no equal found anywhere else throughout the state of Pennsylvania. From the exquisite architecture and craftsmanship to its rich history and multiple community uses, the Scranton Cultural Center at the Masonic Temple has much to offer indeed, even without the prospect of paranormal activity. In addition, psychics and mediums who have walked its halls say there are many secret chambers within the walls and secret rooms within the extensive structure that could store treasures and relics alike. All of this paired with the exciting tales of ghosts and strange activity brings an entire other dimension to the building and makes one wonder what other secrets it could be holding.

8

THE COLONNADE

BOYS WILL BE BOYS, EVEN AFTER DEATH

A large and stately building currently stands on the property located at the corner of Mulberry Street and Jefferson Avenue and dates back to the early 1870s. The looming three-story structure was originally erected as the Victorian mansion home of Colonel Austin B. Blair, who was the son of the once prominent local businessman James Blair. Originally from New Jersey, James Blair moved to Scranton in 1864 and in 1867 helped to organize the Scranton Savings Bank, where he held the positions of director and president for thirty years, until the time of his death in 1897. He was also an original stockholder and a director of the Delaware, Lackawanna and Western Railroad, which provided a means for the successful Pennsylvania anthracite coal business to infiltrate the markets in New York City, as well as upstate New York. He was also one of the original developers of the first street railway in the city. In addition, James Blair took over as director of the First National Bank of Scranton after the death of its previous director, Joseph H. Scranton, in 1872. Mr. Scranton played a large role in the Blair family, becoming an integral part of the city's heritage.

The Blair mansion is located in a part of the city called the lower hill section, which at the time of its construction was the neighborhood of Scranton's first elite families associated with the coal, railroad and, later,

The original Blair house at 401 Jefferson Avenue. *Courtesy of the Lackawanna Historical Society.*

banking businesses. Austin Blair was born in 1838, moved to Scranton with his parents in 1865 and was educated at Princeton University. The young Blair followed his father into the banking business and eventually became first vice-president of the Scranton Savings Bank after working from a starting position of assistant cashier. In 1871, he built his home at 401 Jefferson Avenue, where he raised three children—Jessie, Alice and James Jr.—with his wife, Emma.

Austin Blair died in 1908 and passed ownership of the home and property to his three children. The residence was then converted from its original Victorian appearance to a Neoclassical style in 1910 by his son James Blair Jr., who added the Corinthian columns, triangular pediments and a third floor that still remain today. James and his family resided in the home from then on, and the Blairs became noted for being avid entertainers of the prominent people and families in the city. James's wife, Dorothy, had the reputation of being a grand hostess, and the family frequently arranged large, lavish parties in the third-floor ballroom of the house. Horse-drawn carriages were known to deliver a steady stream of guests to the Blair residence on a regular basis for these events.

A view of Jefferson Avenue with the Blair house shown on the far left, circa early 1900s. *Courtesy of the Lackawanna Historical Society.*

Front view of the Blair house as later remodeled by James Blair Jr. with the third-floor addition. *Courtesy of the Lackawanna Historical Society and the Colonnade.*

Eventually, the property changed hands from the Blair family to the Munchak family in 1951, following the death of James Jr. The new owner, John Munchak, was a funeral director who moved into the home with his wife, Anna. In 1963, the building became the primary source of operations of his mortuary business for at least the following decade. In addition, the second and third floors of the structure were utilized as efficiency apartments. By 1979, the funeral parlor in the home had to be closed due to a conflict with city zoning regulations, which specified that a mortuary could not be operated in a residential neighborhood. From then on, the building was utilized only as a home for the Munchak family and as rental apartments. The building was later purchased in 2006 by Paul Blackledge and Joshua Mast, the present-day owners of the property.

Blackledge and Mast of Posh Life, LLC, completely renovated the house and surrounding property. The house and grounds endured a detailed and historically sensitive two-year metamorphosis to become the lavish and elegant high-class event venue that stands today. Some of the original features of the home were preserved to pay homage to its original glory, but the poor condition of the near-abandoned building and its new proposed use dictated that the majority of its amenities needed to be reworked. Once completed, the level of effort and the results achieved by the current owners were truly an impressive and commendable sight to behold. The pair essentially brought the once grand and beloved structure back from the dead to serve as a bright focal point in the city of Scranton once again. However, their efforts seem to have been noticed by more than just the living people bustling about the city streets today. Some would say that ghosts of the past have also taken a liking to the building and wish to spend time there as well.

It is well known in the field of the paranormal that the act of renovating an existing building can often serve as a catalyst for reviving old spirits lingering in that location. These spirits may be of people who have dwelt in the building or had some other strong connection to the location during their living years. Whatever the case, the spirits seem to sense changes in the location and react in a positive or negative manner by acting out in some way. This in turn often results in the current residents of the building noticing strange occurrences when they did not previously experience anything similar at the location, despite having lived or worked there for many years. In many instances, even the slightest brush with the paranormal, as innocent as it might be, has the potential to be absolutely unnerving to the average person, so living with a spirit can be a delicate situation, to say the very least. However, if a resident spirit is harmless and is accepted and welcomed with an open mind, it can often bring a unique sense of character to a home, business or historic location.

The current owners of the Colonnade experienced this sort of feeling firsthand without ever suspecting it could happen. Their first encounter with a resident spirit of the building occurred very early in the planning stages of the restoration, before any construction work was even started. The project began simply by taking photos of the exterior of the building, an act that is typical of any other historic structure restoration. These photographs were then given to an architect to be used as a background image for a rendering of the proposed building façade. During this stage of planning, the goal was to create a new image for the building that would be a masterful combination of its original Victorian style, later Neoclassical style and the modern contemporary style. The past and the present were to be skillfully melded together to transform the once stately private residence into a beautiful fully functional event hall with bed-and-breakfast capabilities. This new facelift would restore the curb appeal of the building and provide a new breath of life to a long-neglected structure that was in dire need of restoration.

However, something strangely profound happened when the architect examined the photographs of the existing building more closely. No matter what was done to disguise the current look of the original home, in the background there was one feature that could not be masked so easily. It was a piece of the past that stared back from of the image with the eyes of a child. The architect phoned the owners of the structure and asked what to do with the image of the boy in the photograph. Needless to say, the owners were shocked to hear this since they were the ones who had taken the pictures of the building and knew there was no child present in or around the home when the photos were taken. The owners initially thought that the architect was joking about the boy in the photograph, but they had not personally examined the images prior to sending them to be used for the rendering. Sure enough, to their utter surprise, upon inspection of a front view of the building taken from the sidewalk directly across the street, the haunting image of a young boy could be seen standing on a side porch. The dark-haired boy appeared no older than eight or nine years of age and seemed to look directly at the taker of the photograph. In addition, he was oddly dressed in white knickerbockers, or baggy knee-length pants, with white knee-high stockings that were a popular fashion in the late 1800s and early 1900s for men and boys. Even though the owners were sure that no child was present when the picture was taken, the clearly dated attire of the boy in the photo provided an eerie certainty for them that he was not from the modern era.

Since that time, the owners have had several visits from a medium, who perceived the presence of a young male spirit in the building without knowing anything about the structure's former history or the peculiar photograph taken shortly before the restoration. The medium suspected that the child did not die in the home but did reside there for some period during his lifetime. After death, his spirit had returned to 401 Jefferson Avenue because he had fond memories of the home and wanted to stay there forever. This entity is a harmless spirit that possesses the youthful playfulness of a child. He enjoys running though the building and jumping up and down on the beds, especially in the front bedroom on the southern side of the house, which could have been his room when he was alive. The medium revealed that this was evident by the unexplained footsteps sometimes heard throughout the house and the suspicious impressions found from time to time on the surface of the prepared beds.

It is not known who exactly this child spirit was in life, but a distinct possibility could be Austin Blair's son, James Blair Jr., who was born at the home in 1872 and was responsible for remodeling the house in 1910. This theory, although atypical, may be plausible. James Blair Jr. lived well beyond youth and died in 1950 at the age of seventy-eight. Perhaps James

Jr.'s impression of heaven was to return to the home he loved as a child so he could play and frolic there for all eternity. In addition, the clothing of the boy in the photo would certainly fit the era when James Jr. was a young lad. Another strange coincidence is that the image of the boy in the photograph is seen standing on the side porch of the home, which was removed during the restoration process to make way for the new addition that houses the main dining area and kitchen of the Colonnade. Could the spirit have suspected the removal of this feature in advance of the project planning and was displaying his opposition by standing there?

Another possibility is that the presence of the boy in the building is only the imprint of the child's residual energy, which was absorbed into the very fabric of the home. A residual haunting is an imprint of energy that can periodically play back a past event or series of events at a location under the right conditions and is often mistaken for an actual spirit when seen or heard. However, these imprints are only a trace aspect of the associated individual and not a complete intelligent entity that can interact and communicate with the living. Usually in hauntings, residual energy is believed to come from or be linked to a traumatic or negative event, like a sudden tragic death or murder. On the other hand, positive imprints such as the energy created from the joyous experiences of a young boy raised by a good and loving family could also linger in a location if proven strong enough.

Still another explanation may be provided by the use of the building as a funeral home. Perhaps the spirit haunting the Colonnade originated from an unfortunate child who had his final preparations for interment while in the building. However, this theory seems unlikely for this particular ghost based on the early twentieth-century clothing present in the photograph and the fact that the building did not become a funeral parlor until the 1960s.

Until more evidence comes to light, it may never be known who or what haunts the former Blair house. Whatever the truth is behind the ghostly presence in the building, the Colonnade certainly remains an exquisite asset to present-day Scranton while simultaneously playing tribute to the glorious history of the city. After all, where else could one go that is so equally adored by the dead as well as the living?

9

THE ELECTRIC CITY TROLLEY MUSEUM

HAUNTED CAR #46

Some buildings can be haunted, not because of the history of the location itself, but because of the history of the items inside. The same can be said of the Electric City Trolley Museum, which stands at 300 Cliff Street. The building that currently houses the museum was erected in 1877 and was originally composed of two separate buildings owned and operated by the Dickson Manufacturing Company. The original buildings were destroyed by fire in 1874, but this site was the previous location of the Cliff Works Engine Manufacturing Company, which was purchased by the Dickson Manufacturing Company in 1862. The Dickson Manufacturing Company was the maker of locomotives and stationary steam engines. The present Electric City Trolley Museum building once housed a machine shop for that business. The company started out small, with only 30 employees, but began to thrive and grow exponentially since the machinery and parts it produced supported all the major industries of Scranton at that time. By the late 1890s, the Dickson Manufacturing Company was 1,200 employees strong, produced around one hundred locomotives a year and supplied its products to the entire nation.

Eventually, the property became involved in a series of acquisitions by a number of other various businesses throughout the years. In 1912,

The original buildings located on the site of the present-day Electric City Trolley Museum at 300 Cliff Street. *Courtesy of the Lackawanna Historical Society.*

the Scranton Silk Mill Company purchased the north building, and the south building was purchased in 1914 by the Maccar Truck Company, which later became known as Mack Trucks. The Williams Baking Company then purchased the north building in 1921 and used it as a warehouse for its baked goods. When the silk mill closed in 1936, Williams also bought the south building, adapted it for storage and connected the two buildings. Scranton Dry Goods, a prominent city department store, purchased the building in 1956 and later sold it to be used for furniture storage until 1979. Most recently, the property became part of the adjacent Steamtown National Historic Site, which was established in 1984 on the original DL&W rail yards. In 1999, following extensive documentation, restoration and reconstruction, the facility was opened to the public by Lackawanna County as the Electric City Trolley Museum.

The old silk mill building currently serves as the museum's interpretive center, where one can learn about the history of the early Pennsylvania electric trolley lines and about the construction and workings of the cars themselves. The electric trolley is an important aspect in describing the past innovations and successes of Scranton, Pennsylvania, and from where it's nickname, the "Electric City," originated. On November 30, 1886, the first commercially viable electrically operated streetcar in the nation was run along Franklin Avenue from the corner of Lackawanna Avenue to the Green Ridge Section of Scranton. At that time, electric power was a truly technical marvel, and the trolley system helped to solve an increasing transit problem in the city. The sixteen-foot-long streetcars could seat up to twenty-six passengers and soon replaced the original horse-drawn trolleys, which cost five times the amount of money to operate. In addition, the newer cars provided a traveler with comfort and were lit on the interior with incandescent electric lamps. Eventually, the electric trolleys for passenger use declined in Scranton and completely ended in 1954.

The remainder of the museum building houses several vintage trolley cars for display and educational purposes. It is here where one of these cars possesses a macabre history of its very own and where our true ghostly tale begins. The infamous Car #46 is a double-truck, double-end, closed car and one of twenty-two similar cars built in 1907 by the St. Louis Car Company, which operated on the Philadelphia and Western Railway. It is the last remaining car representing this first generation of trolley cars to run on a high-standard third-rail system from the Sixty-ninth Street Terminal in Upper Darby, Pennsylvania, to Strafford, with a later branch to Norristown. The third-rail system pertains to the technique of current distribution for the operation of the cars dating back to at least 1893. The third rail was an insulator

Trolley Car #46, built in 1907 by the St. Louis Car Company. It was used to run from the Sixty-ninth Street Terminal in Upper Darby, Pennsylvania, to Strafford, Pennsylvania. The car is believed to be haunted by the ghost of a female passenger who died on the car in 1908. The car is currently restored and on display at the Electric City Trolley Museum. *Courtesy of the Don Ross Group.*

made of wood, stoneware, semi-porcelain, reconstructed granite and, later, total porcelain; it housed the power source that ran the cars and was located alongside or between the rails of the railway track.

Great pride and craftsmanship went into the construction of these classic interurban-style cars, which were primarily constructed of wood with steel under body frames. Each car was fitted with beautiful arched stained-glass windows and ornate interior woodworking. Car #46 has only survived to the present day because it was converted into a work car, renamed as #446, in 1928 and was in operation until its retirement in 1976. The museum obtained the car sometime later and put it on display in the building. The car's exterior appearance has been restored back to its original elegance, and the once-detailed interior is presently also being restored.

The legend of Car #46 originates back in the early 1900s, when the car itself was brand new and being utilized for passenger transportation in the southeastern portion of Pennsylvania. A young woman in her late twenties was seated toward the rear of the car. She was traveling the route alone on an urgent expedition to reach family members in the Philadelphia area. The trip at this time and location in history should have been a pleasant one given the comfort and beautiful craftsmanship of the trolley car and the convenient and exciting new method of transportation. However, Nancy, as she later became known by the staff at the Electric City Trolley Museum, was gravely ill, and her life was rapidly fleeting away from moment to moment like grains of sand passing through an hourglass. Nancy was severely weakened by her illness and desperately trying to reach the comfort of her family in Philadelphia, where she could seek out more advanced medical treatments and hopefully regain her health. Unfortunately, the young woman's desires did not come to fruition because at some point along the route she sadly was overcome by her illness and did not reach her final destination alive. It is believed that while seated, she quietly slipped into unconsciousness and died, perhaps without anyone on the trolley noticing until the end of the trip, when she failed to rise from her seat and exit the car.

After all this time, it seems the extreme and desperate nature of the trip, and the great desire to reach her family members, has burned within her soul long after the black veil of death descended on her body. Nancy's

Trolley Car #46 as later converted to work car #446. *Courtesy of the Don Ross Group.*

spirit is said to have lingered in Car #46 long after her death in 1908. This tragic tale is a reality to some of the staff members of the Electric City Trolley Museum who have experienced a good amount of unexplained paranormal phenomena in the building in and around Car #46 since its addition to the museum in 1999.

Just try to imagine for a moment how awfully daunting, tedious and frustrating it would be to exist in a trolley car for over one hundred years without knowing how to get out or why the other people on the car can't see or hear you. It would truly seem like hell to most people and would make one wonder what this poor woman did to deserve such an unfortunate turn of events. Dying at such a young age would certainly be bad enough without the prospect of one's spirit being trapped in such a small space for that long. However, it has been theorized that the dead perceive time in a different manner because their consciousness, or awareness, is no longer bound by the rules of the living world or a living body. A living person perceives the passage of time to be linear—time flows from moment to moment like a stream flows past a tree or some other stationary object. This happens for a number of reasons, including our internal biological clocks, our observance of changes in the world and our expectations of those changes. For the dead, this linear perception of time is removed when the body dies; therefore, the past, present and future all exist as one singular entity. Time no longer flows forward and hence is perceived in its true nature or form. Hopefully, this reality may have provided a way for Nancy's spirit to not perceive the passage of nearly 104 years, even as the outside world and the use of the trolley car itself changed around her. It is doubtful that Nancy did anything to deserve this unfortunate sentence, but her spirit simply refused to pass on to the next level of existence due to her unfinished business and strong will to remain in the world of the living. Because of this, her spirit became trapped in between worlds, and Car #46 became a literal cell where she has been a prisoner.

Many skeptics would think this could not happen, but the eerie reality is that some staff members, as well as many visitors to the museum, have claimed to experience feelings of uneasiness or dread and have heard disembodied voices when near Car #46. More often than he would like, a male maintenance employee of the museum has reported specifically hearing his name being called out by a woman's voice after-hours when he was alone in the building. The source of the voice is most often traced to Car #46, and no one is present in or near the car upon investigation. Staff members have also reported hearing the sudden and alarming sounds of heavy doors sliding and slamming shut, echoing throughout the darkened museum after it is closed to the public. Perhaps this is Nancy calling out for help or trying to gain the attention of anyone nearby. In addition, while visiting the museum, gifted mediums, clairvoyants and people with developed psychic abilities have claimed to see, or picture, the image of a lone woman sitting in the rear of the car. On one occasion, when the spirit was directly questioned as to whether she was trapped in the car and desired to leave, a disembodied, but loud, "sigh" was heard within Car #46. Even though actual documented evidence of a woman named Nancy dying on Car #46 in 1908 has not yet been officially produced, the legend still holds some shocking credibility due to the personal experiences and paranormal evidence obtained surrounding the legend.

However, poor Nancy may not be the only spirit residing in the museum. Visitors and staff have also had similar experiences in the room adjacent to where Car #46 is now located, near the statues of an early 1900s coal miner and a breaker boy. Mediums have also had contact with a male spirit that is said to roam free about the building; he was supposedly one of the original builders of Car #46. This spirit appears to enjoy surprising or tricking the staff members of the museum by moving certain retail items on the front desk to other areas of the building without explanation. A trip to the Electric City Trolley Museum would indeed provide one with a rich educational experience regarding the history of electric streetcars. However, aside from this, the possibility that the museum still houses actual spirits from that past truly would make a visit even more exciting and unique.

CONCLUSION

Needless to say, my journey over the last eleven years exploring the possibility of life after death and the existence of ghosts has been extremely interesting, exciting and rewarding. Even though I probably have more questions now regarding the paranormal than when I first started, I have witnessed enough during my paranormal investigations and the time spent in review of evidence obtained during those investigations to evolve from a keenly interested skeptic to a firm believer in the spirit world. From a skeptic's point of view, I admit that spending countless hours in supposedly "haunted" locations using image- and audio-capturing equipment and asking questions out loud to only the surrounding darkness would seem to be a definite waste of time and possibly grounds to question of one's sanity. However, I can also say that with an honest, thoughtful approach and an open mind, unexplained evidence of the paranormal can be captured under circumstances that are not just mere coincidence. I have endured numerous strange and unexplained personal experiences and obtained startling evidence from many of my Scranton investigations, including at the Catlin House, Andy Gavin's Eatery and Pub, the Banshee Pub, the Hotel Jermyn, the Colonnade and the Scranton Cultural Center, which I declare are paranormal in nature. The following are but a few examples.

While in the basement of the Banshee Pub, I attest to having experienced feelings of dread and sudden unexplained drops in temperature and witnessing strange moving shadows. There were also many suspicious, unexplained equipment failures, such as instant battery drains on multiple cameras and an audio recorder that would not operate in the basement but worked fine afterward on the other floors of the building. This sort of thing is known to happen to electronic equipment when a nearby spirit is manifesting, trying to communicate or just wants to interfere with an investigation. I also had a significant experience in September 2008 while alone and in total darkness in the vault area of the basement. It was after the bar was closed, and I was sitting in a chair in total silence just listening for anything out of the ordinary. After about fifteen long minutes of this, I remember stating out loud, "There is really no one down here with me." Immediately after uttering this statement, I felt a strong nearby presence and witnessed a form darker than the surrounding space step directly in front of me. Several tense moments passed as I remained totally still but braced myself for anything. Suddenly, I was shocked to feel something like an extended finger slowly brush against the entire length of my exposed right forearm, which was propped on the arm of the chair. I became instantly convinced that I was indeed not alone at that point. This chilling event was only the beginning of the strange occurrences experienced both during the investigation and collected from the analyzed evidence afterward.

During the same investigation, video footage of a glowing orb of light was captured coming out from underneath a table in the second-floor banquet room. The orb slowly floats across the screen and then follows the line of the staircase to the third floor. The most shocking part turned out to be the additional audio evidence, which was captured on the third floor of the building about ten minutes after the orb is seen ascending the staircase on the video. This additional evidence was collected on a digital audio recorder by another investigator who was on the third floor at the time; it eerily resembled the high-pitched voice of a young girl saying the word "please." Ironically, that staircase is the exact location where the employee interviewed in 2008 saw the image of the young girl whose spirit is believed to haunt the building. However, this was only a small part of the striking audio evidence collected from the building during both 2008 investigations, which totaled more than thirty recordings with up to five different voices, some male and some female. The voices provided some concise answers to specific questions asked by the investigators and revealed information about the history of the location and their presence in the building.

To my surprise, many of the other historic locations in downtown Scranton contained spirits just waiting to communicate with someone who wants to listen. While in the now-defunct theater located in the Hotel Jermyn, I had a strange experience behind the stage, which I later found out was the act of a spirit trying to get my attention. It was very early into the investigation, and I sat alone in a chair in total darkness behind the stage with my hand-held video recorder set up close by on a table facing me and another stationary video camera on a tripod farther away to capture a much larger portion of the backstage area. I relaxed and began to think of questions to ask Eleanor, the spirit of the female performer who is believed to haunt the theater area of the building. After years of investigating, I have learned to become less dependent on the equipment and more in tune with my instincts, senses and feelings to hone in on the location of possible nearby spirit entities. For instance, that specific area behind the stage, or perhaps the very chair I was sitting in, seemed to call out and draw me in, so I decided to start the investigation there and not ignore the location's significance to me. I soon began to ask the questions that appeared in my mind regarding the history of the building and the tale of Eleanor to hopefully provoke some response. Suddenly, I noticed that the freshly charged hand-held video camera operating directly in front of me shut off by itself. I glanced around, slowly turned the camera back on and continued the session without any further interruption.

I was later astounded upon viewing the footage obtained from the stationary camera. It captured a disembodied female voice, which exclaimed, "Yoo-hoo!" just after the hand-held camera is seen shutting off by itself while I'm looking around for an explanation. I did not hear the voice at the time, even though it was captured on the camera, but this is very common with electronic voice phenomena (EVP) since it can occur simultaneously with another background noise, and the human mind has a tendency to tune out spirit voices and associated "white" noise.

I was astounded even further when I did a walk-through of the theater with a very talented local clairvoyant medium named Lady Tara Lee a few weeks after the investigation to see what she could pick up on and whether it correlated to my knowledge of the location. Without knowing anything regarding the history of the building, the known ghost stories or any details of my previous investigation, she was able to provide me with accurate information about the lingering spirit of the female performer, the death of the carpenter during the construction of the building and the local priest with a love of theater who had died from a heart attack in the building several years ago. In addition, as Lady Tara sat in the exact same chair backstage where I had sat during my investigation, she informed me that the spirit of a female performer who died of foul play in the building in the 1930s was present at the time of my investigation and that this spirit was the one who shut the camera off and had called out "Yoo-hoo!" to get my attention. I was literally floored since up until that point I had not told her about the spirit named Eleanor or the voice I had captured at that very location during my investigation.

Lady Tara Lee is a naturally gifted, formally trained ordained spiritualist minister and certified medium who began to sense spirits around the age of two. She is also a personal friend of mine and has assisted me on numerous successful paranormal investigations where her knowledge and intuition provided information vital to those cases. She is an all-around great person who is legitimately concerned with the well-being of others, whether alive or dead.

In terms of history, ghosts can serve as a possible link to the past and sometimes assist the living in discovering certain underlying truths regarding events that were previously forgotten, unknown or altered over time. For instance, it is extremely interesting and exciting to gain random information of a location or person through contact with a "spirit" during a paranormal investigation and later realize through research that the collected information correlates very closely with the known history regarding that specific person or location. The above scenario is certainly quite thought-provoking and is difficult to chalk up to mere coincidence.

However, I have found out firsthand that this sort of phenomenon can and does happen once one delves seriously into the realm of paranormal investigation. The idea of spirits lingering in the world of the living and passing on historically accurate information can be mind/life altering and even frightening to most people. Conversely, for the unrattled minority out there possessing the will and resolve to dig deeper, the knowledge gained can provide additional understanding of the hidden world around us and possibly a renewed faith or spirituality.

I am very pleased to have had the opportunity to pass on some of my knowledge and experiences to you. Perhaps in a future volume I can discuss some of the other spiritually active locations in the city of Scranton, such as the Everhart Museum, which is supposedly haunted by its creator, Dr. Isaiah Fawkes Everhart, who donated the new building to the city as a gift in 1908 and later died inside after a tragic fall, as well as the surrounding Nay Aug Park, which is reputably haunted by the souls of the numerous people who died swimming in the nearby natural gorge area over the years. In any event, I hope all of you arm-chair adventurers out there found this book to be entertaining and maybe even a little enlightening. However, I encourage you braver souls to visit some or all of the locations discussed in this book and/or other known haunted locations to gain a further appreciation of the history behind them and possibly to experience something supernatural yourself. The spirit world is closer than you think, and whether or not you believe it, the unseen ghosts of the past exist and can be standing right next to you just waiting for the chance to be heard.

BIBLIOGRAPHY

Adams, Charles J., III. *Luzerne and Lackawanna Counties Ghosts Legends & Lore*. Wyomissing, PA: Exeter House Books, 2007.

Burton, Jeremy G. "Ghost Walk Tours Scranton's Macabre Past." *Times-Tribune*, October 18, 2009.

Castillo, Stephanie. "A Walk on the Dark Side." *Weekender*, October 14, 2009.

Colonnade. www.thecolonnade401.com.

Electric City Trolley Museum Association. www.ectma.org.

Falchek, David. "Paranormal Investigators Look into Downtown Scranton." *Times-Tribune*, October 18, 2010.

Hitchcock, Frederick L. *History of Scranton and Its People*. 2 vols. New York: Lewis Historical Pub. Co., 1914.

Hollister, H., MD. *History of the Lackawanna Valley with Illustrations*. 5th ed., revised and enlarged. Philadelphia: J.B. Lippincott Company, 1885.

Kashuba, Cheryl A. *A Brief History of Scranton, Pennsylvania.* Charleston, SC: The History Press, 2009.

Lackawanna County. www.lackawannacounty.org.

Lackawanna Historical Society. www.lackawannahistory.org.

Lackawanna Historical Society Newsletter 5, no. 3 (January–February 1971).

Lady Tara Lee. www.ladytaralee.com.

Lynch, Eileen A. "The Flu of 1918." *Pennsylvania Gazette,* October 28, 1998.

McCauley, Scott D. " A Room with a Boo!" *Is This Thing On?* June 25, 2009.

Peck, George, DD. *Wyoming: Its History, Stirring Incidents, and Romantic Adventures.* New York: Harper & Brothers, Publishers, 1858.

Pennsylvania Haunts and History. www.hauntsandhistory.blogspot.com.

Radisson Lackawanna Station Hotel. www.radisson.com.

Scranton City Directory. 1879–1880. Lackawanna Historical Society, Scranton, Pennsylvania.

Scranton Cultural Center at the Masonic Temple. www.scrantonculturalcenter.org.

Scranton Times. "Death of Mrs. Catlin Releases Property to Historical Group." April 15, 1942.

ABOUT THE AUTHOR

A.C. Bernardi is a licensed professional civil engineer who was born in Scranton, Pennsylvania, and is employed at CECO Associates, Inc., Consulting Engineers, whose office is located within the heart of the downtown area. He's also the founder/lead investigator of the Scranton After Dark Paranormal Society (SADPS), an active member and volunteer of the Lackawanna Historical Society (LHS) and on the board of directors for the Anthracite Heritage Society & Iron Furnaces

Author A.C. Bernardi in front of the Brooks Model Coal Mine entrance at Nay Aug Park in Scranton, Pennsylvania. *Photo by Olivia Bernardi.*

Associates. Through historical research and his own documented experiences during actual paranormal investigations of the local haunted sites, Mr. Bernardi developed the script for "Scranton After Dark: A Walk Through Haunted History," which has been a successful fundraiser for the LHS since the fall of 2009. He grew up just minutes from the Scranton area and graduated from Abington Heights High School. Mr. Bernardi has a bachelor's of science degree in civil engineering from Pennsylvania State University and lives in South Abington Township with his wife, Olivia; three children, Evan, Owen and Gwen; his dog, Sugar; and his cat, Avon.

Visit us at
www.historypress.net

....

This title is also available as an e-book